D0557721

Harsh Weather
CAMPING

Also by the author:

Whitewater!, by Norman Strung, Sam Curtis and Earl Perry

Harsh Weather
CAMPING

Sam Curtis

Menasha Ridge Press
Birmingham, Alabama

Acknowledgments

Thanks to the following suppliers for permission to use their photographs:
Katadyn U.S.A., Inc., 3020 N. Scottsdale Rd., Scottsdale, AZ 85251
Northern Outfitters, 1083 N. State St., Orem, UT 84057
Old Town Canoe, Old Town, Maine 04468
Performance Bike Shop, 88=PBS=BIKE, P. O. Box 2741, Chapel Hill,
NC 27514
Recreational Equipment, Inc., 800=426=4849, P. O. Box 88125, Seattle,
WA 98138=2125

Published by Menasha Ridge Press
3169 Cahaba Heights Road
Birmingham, AL 35243

Second edition, first printing, 1993

Library of Congress Cataloging in Publication Data:

Curtis, Sam.
Harsh Weather Camping
        Reprint. Originally published: New York: D, McKay Co.,
c1980.
        Included index.
        1. Camping. 2. Camping - Equipment and supplies.
I Title.
[GV191.7.C87   1983]   688.7'679654   83-7240
ISBN 0-89732-133-2

Printed in the United States of America.

To Alice and Gould Curtis

who, among other things,
helped me understand that a rainy day
is mainly a state of mind.

Contents

Introduction

"A book on camping in crummy weather! Why in the world do you want to write about that?"

That response represents the bewilderment expressed by some of my more indoor-oriented friends upon hearing of the plans for this book. And, I suppose harsh weather is not usually the first thing to come to mind when thinking of the possible joys of backpacking, bicycling, or canoeing. The question, however, suggests a basic disbelief in the possibility of enjoying any of these activities in the teeth of heart, cold, or moisture.

There was a time when I harbored the same disbelief.

The specific episode that comes to mind happened during my adolescence. It was a May weekend in Connecticut, and my friend Clifford and I had spent the better part of the school week intent on camping plans instead of homework. As is typical of spring in the Northeast, Saturday dawned drab and dreary. Clouds hung on the branches of maples in the yard, and the humidity could be measured with a ladle. But we would not be deterred from our plans. And off we trudged under a knowing parental gaze.

Outfitted à la Army Surplus, we felt sure that a bit of rain could not inundate our optimistic mood. And we probably would have been right had we not underestimated the rain.

The dousing started in a fine spray that filtered through the walls. But by the time the wind had pulled out several tent pegs and we had pawed the canvas shelter halves back into place, the deluge was almost complete. All we needed was the pond that developed around the down filling of our olive-drab sleeping bags. We spent the rest of the night, and a considerable number of years thereafter, muttering over the miseries of foul-weather camping.

A lot has changed since then. Some of the changes are in personal experience and know-how in coping with the outdoors, but a great deal of the most significant changes have taken place in the materials and designs of outdoor clothing and equipment. In fact, it's ironic that the complexities of contemporary technology have provided us with the gear that enables us to live simply but comfortably in weather we never dreamed of camping in before, weather that in former years not only tested but also usually went beyond the limits of our camping capabilities.

"Be that as it may," my skeptical acquaintances will counter, "who wants to go camping in heat, cold, or foggy, foggy dew to begin with?"

It's clear that many people do no want to go camping in bad weather. Yet thousands get caught every year by unexpected rain storms, snow squalls, and heat waves. That is one good reason for a book that deals with the nuances of coping with harsh weather, even if the rain wasn't asked for, the snow wasn't wanted, or the dog days weren't included in the plans.

Besides, a significant and growing number of hikers, bikers, and canoeists actually *choose* to go out in harsh weather. For some of them, rain is a part of exploring Pacific Coast beaches or of catching the best fall colors in New England. Other campers put up with dry heat in search of Navaho ruins or with wet heat in pursuit of Florida bass. And some campers never sleep more snugly than when dug into a snow cave at 10,000 feet, or who ski out into the cold to find the stark, elemental beauty that only winter can create. Some campers simply find their favorite trails pleasantly uncluttered when certain quirks of nature send these hordes of fair-weather campers scurrying home.

Although much of the talk in Harsh-Weather Camping is about the current state of the art in clothing, equipment, and technique, the purpose of it all is to let you get out in any kind of weather and have fun. The information is meant to help you enjoy doing and seeing things. It isn't intended to make you so myopically involved in keeping cool or dry or warm that you don't get a thrill out of a whitewater run in the rain or don't admire the waxy red of a cactus blooming at your feet or don't notice the beauty of a snow-covered fir. In other words, this book is about not merely surviving in harsh weather but also enjoying the great outdoors under widely varying conditions. Read the book with this idea in mind. I'll remind you of it from time to time.

Preface to Second Edition

In the decade since the first edition of *Harsh Weather Camping*, the biggest change of import for harsh weather campers has been the advent of "technical fabrics" and their use in "clothing systems." Where natural fibers like wool, cotton, and silk once formed the stuff of outdoor clothing, now synthetic fibers—especially polypropylene and polyester—flex their man-made muscles.

Synthetics were around a decade ago, but they've gone through a lot of changes. They've been made into new fiber configurations; they've been plucked, stretched, and tweaked. They've been modified chemically, molecularly, and physically. In other words, they've become *technical* fabrics that numerous manufacturers and outfitters have put into clothing systems. You can now get an item-compatible outdoor wardrobe—everything from underwear to outer shell—from any number of brand name suppliers.

These clothing systems are intended to pull unwanted moisture away from your body, push it through all the layers of clothing, and vent it to the outside air without letting rain or snow back in. It's a nice trick if you can do it, and modern technology, along with efficient design and construction, has succeeded to varying degrees.

I have not gone head over tail feathers for hi-tech. I still believe that "when it ain't broke, ya' don't fix it." So, for the 1990's, I recommend a blend of traditional, field-tested gear, the best of the hi-tech, and a good dose of old *and* new ways to use what you take on the trail.

BOZEMAN, MONTANA
1991

SECTION I

Camping
in the Rain

1

Wet-Weather Wise

It's the evening before a planned trip to Shenandoah National Park or perhaps Point Reyes National Seashore. As you stuff a bag of dry-roasted cashews into the upper left-hand pocket of your pack, the voice of Sandra the weather lady bores into your consciousness.

". . . . winds from the south southeast at 8 miles per hour . . . moving a low pressure system in from the west . . . A look at our weather-satellite picture shows what's in store for the next few days . . . There's a 40 percent chance of measurable precip tonight, increasing to 60 percent by tomorrow . . . Coming up next, Harry with the. . . ."

Rain!

Should you cancel the trip? It's been planned for weeks. Hiking when it's wet is such a drag. You could stay home and sleep for three days. Why did it have to come now? You knew this would happen when George made you put off the trip for a week. Remember how wet your boots got on that Buckeye Trail trip? Probably happen again this time.

The expectation of rain is as much a part of most campers' psychic energy as listening for things that go bump in the night. For many people, worrying about rain is actually more preoccupying than dealing with it when it arrives. All this concern about weather, however, is typically accompanied by the fatalistic notion that nothing can be

3

done about it. While it's true that you can't stop rain from falling, things *can* be done to prepare yourself for coping with it comfortably.

Under certain conditions, whether you stay dry in wet weather can be a matter of personal choice. A light drizzle in a warm temperature may call for nothing more than a philosophical shrug as you continue

Recreational Equipment, Inc.

The expectation of rain is as much a part of most campers'
psychic energy as listening for things that go bump in the night.

to paddle. A day of this kind of precipitation, called "dry rain" in the northwest, can leave you feeling no more than a bit humidified. But even an afternoon thunderstorm, as torrential as it can be, may seem providential if you happen to be hiking in a scorching spot like Arizona's Ajo Mountains in the summer. The point is that rain in many forms under a variety of circumstances may trigger wet-headed celebrations instead of concerned scramblings for foul-weather clothing.

At other times, though, getting wet can range in consequence from feeling slightly mildewed to becoming dangerously like a brass statue on a cold day. Rain that verges on falling slush can turn an autumn or spring hike amidst Wisconsin's hardwoods into something akin to a ramble through an ice-cream machine, if you don't have the clothes to suit the situation. Likewise, wind-driven rain, even in mild temperatures, will find its way through all but the most watertight apparel and will bring on the teeth-chattering chills. Consequently, an awareness of impending weather is a basic concern for any camper. And since no other weather is as varied as the wet kind, there is no other time when it is more important for you to be weather wise. Only then will you know whether to take a tarp or a mountain tent, or whether to air your sleeping bag on a bush or stuff into a sack.

Pre-Trip Weather Information

Checking on the weather before you set out on a trip is sometimes simply a matter of listening to the long-range (five-day) forecast. That's what the meteorologists are in business for. And despite our frequent skepticism about the know-how, they're the best source we have.

When you are trying to plan for a trip in country you're not familiar with, it's a different matter. You've got to know, long before you leave home, what general climatic conditions to expect for the time of year. Two sources are indispensable for this kind of planning:

(1) *The Climatic Atlas of the U.S.* provides statistics from across the country that cover average and extreme temperatures, precipitation, wind, barometric pressure, relative humidity, dew point, sunshine, sky cover, solar radiation, and evaporation. It's available for $4.25 from Superintendent of Documents, U.S. Government Printing Office, Washington, D.C. 20402.

(2) If you are interested in only one state, however, you can write to The National Climatic Center, Federal Building, Asheville, North Carolina 28801, and ask for a Climatic Survey of your chosen state. The cost varies but the booklet will include information on a monthly

precipitation and temperatures.

With either of these sources you might find it helpful to discover, for example, that summers in Maine can be cool and moist with storms at any time. Or that the first frost in northern Wisconsin is usually in September. Or that Arizona's wettest season is June through August. This kind of information can go a long way toward basic take-it-or-leave-it-at-home planning.

Forecasting Weather on the Trail

Keeping tabs on the weather while on route is just as important as knowing what to expect before you leave home. Canoeing across an open stretch of water can be safe and even comfortable in a light rain. But if you know heavy winds are likely to arise, you can delay your crossing until a more favorable time. Similarly, hikers who are able to predict a brewing electrical storm can avoid summits and high passes where exposure to lightning is greatest (see Chapter 4). In many other situations, knowing what to expect of the weather will help keep you both comfortable and safe.

The best weather source on a trip is a battery powered weather-band radio. Radio Shack® has one that measures roughly 4 x 5 inches and weighs 11 ounces. It broadcasts continuously, giving complete weather updates approximately every four hours, and gives emergency weather alerts immediately.

In the absence of a weather radio, the best approach to forecasting the weather is through observation of clouds and wind direction. Inexpensive books and booklets, such as Instant Weather Forecasting and Pocket Weather Trends, use these indicators in photo and chart form to predict weather 12 to 36 hours in advance. As handy as these devices are, learning to read clouds and observe wind direction on your own will make you more self-sufficient on the trail and probably more in tune with important weather changes.

Clouds As Weather Indicators

Man has been watching the skies for centuries. Long before the advent of sophisticated weather instruments, outdoor people have been able to predict rain or shine through changes in cloud formations. In many instances, proverbs have evolved around these weather phenomena and what they suggest. I've found the factually based proverbs a handy way to remember what various cloud formations and cloud progressions indicate about upcoming weather.

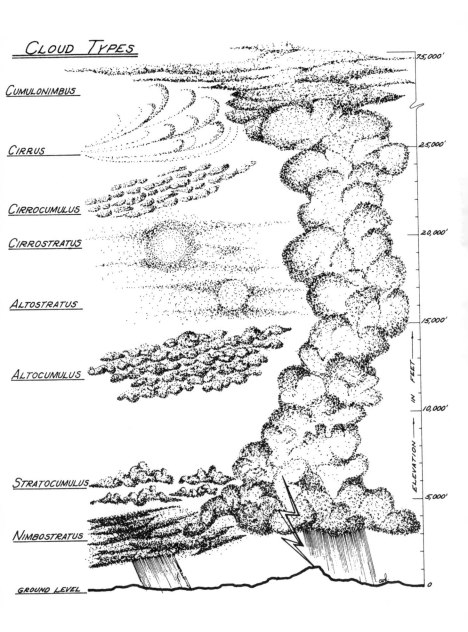

Observation of cloud types and their progression from one kind to another can help you forecast weather.

There are two general classes of clouds that are distinguished by their shape.

• *Cumulus* clouds are the puffy ones that resemble an accumulation of cottonballs.

• *Stratus* clouds are stratified in sheetlike layers.

Clouds are further classified according to height. The general progression of clouds that can be counted on to bring rain (or snow when it's cold) will move from high altitudes to low ones. The faster this progression occurs, the quicker the rain will pass. The longer the change takes, the more drawn-out the rain will be.

> Short notice, soon to pass;
> Long notice, long 'twill last.

High Clouds

• *Cirrus*—These are the high whispy clouds, often called mares' tails, that are composed of ice crystals. By themselves, cirrus clouds don't necessarily portend rainy weather, but if they are followed by lowered and increasing cloudiness, a warm front and rain is probably on the way.

• *Cirrostratus*—These are the clouds that look like thin layers of gauze. The refraction of light by ice crystals in cirrostratus clouds gives the sun or moon a definite halo. Consequently, this saying will make sense when the appearance of a halo is followed by lower, thicker clouds.

> When a halo rings the moon or sun
> The rain will come upon the run.

• *Cirrocumulus*—Consisting of a series of small puffs that seem to come in waves, these clouds are said to look like mackerel scales. Because both cirrocumulus and cirrus clouds are often the first indicators of high-altitude winds that are bringing in a storm, the following proverb may help you remember them as clues.

> Mackerel scales and mares' tails
> Make lofty ships carry low sails.

Middle-Level Clouds

Altostratus and altocumulus are the clouds likely to follow high-level clouds when rain is on the way.

• *Altostratus*—These are the clouds that look like a thick grey sheet through which the sun or moon seems fuzzy, as if seen through etched glass.

• *Altocumulus*—Altocumulus clouds come in blotchy patches with grey centers and will often form into lines. The sun or moon shining through this formation will be closely surrounded by a faint rainbow-like light.

When either altostratus or altocumulus start to form and thicken, rain will probably arrive within 6 to 8 hours.

Low-Level Clouds

• *Stratocumulus*—These patchy or continuous layers of round clouds with flattened bases form low in the sky and may spit some rain or snow.

• *Nimbostratus*—Nimbostratus are the true rain cloud. They are thick and dark grey and usually bring a long, steady rain.

Once on a northern canoe trip, we'd been paddling in the face of lowering clouds all day. By 4 p.m. the wind quickened and the sky darkened appreciably under the shadow of nimbostratus clouds. It was clearly time to get off the lake.

Setting up camp was a race against the rain, which we could see moving down on us as we pounded the last tent pegs into place. We ended up piling into the tent with our gear at about the same time the first heavy drops broke across our rainfly. It was clearly a case of close-call forecasting.

Thunderheads

Although a prolonged rain is usually associated with a progression of high-to-middle-to-low-level clouds, thunderstorms develop in a different way. Cumulus clouds, scattered and billowy, are typical of fair weather unless they begin to collect and develop upward. Then they form into the cumulonimbus clouds most of us know as thunderheads. These may bring heavy rains and sometimes hail (because they can build to the chilling height of 75,000 feet), but the rains usually don't last very long.

Wind as Weather Indicator

As important as clouds are in predicting weather changes, winds also play a major role. Wind direction and shifts in wind direction taken in association with cloud changes will give you an even more accurate idea of what weather to expect.

Important in understanding the influence of winds is the fact that prevailing winds in most of the U.S. move from west to east. These are called the prevailing westerlies, and it is from the west that you should usually look for weather changes. For example, if the western sky is dark with low nimbostratus clouds, it's a good bet your Spanish Rice will get watered down if the cooking pot isn't covered.

But the winds can be deceptive. High-pressure and low-pressure systems are responsible for this complication. On a barometer (which is simply an air-weighing device), cold dry air registers a higher reading than warm wet air, which weighs less. So large air masses of cold dry air are called highs, and masses of warm moist air are called lows. Highs are associated with fair weather, lows with poor weather.

As high-pressure systems are blown across the northern hemisphere from west to east by prevailing westerlies, they rotate in a clockwise direction. If you picture this situation in your mind's eye, you will realize that a wind from the north often indicates the leading edge of a high and the advent of good weather. Low-pressure systems, on the other hand, rotate in a counterclockwise direction. With that picture in your mind's eye, you will realize that the leading edge of these poor-weather systems will come in on a south wind:

> When the wind is in the South,
> The rain is in its mouth.

As the low-pressure system passes, it will produce winds that shift from the south to the north and northwest. These winds may blow for several days, dropping at sunset and rising again by mid-morning. They can be particularly hazardous for canoeists who misinterpret the morning calm as a permanent condition.

As a general rule, you can associate winds that are shifting in a counterclockwise direction with poor weather and winds shifting clockwise with fair weather. In addition, south, east, and northeast winds suggest coming precipitation; north, northwest, and southwest winds indicate fair weather.

However, don't mistake local breezes, such as mountain and sea breezes, for the general flow of air in your area. When air is warmed it expands and becomes lighter. Since the sun warms mountain tops faster than valleys, daytime breezes in mountainous areas move *up-slope*. But since the peaks also lose heat faster than the valleys at night, the trend reverses. After sunset, downslope breezes are natural. A similar situation exists around large bodies of water, including the Great Lakes. The sun warms land faster than water, but land also cools faster than water at night. The result is that you will usually get a breeze off the water during the day and off the land at night. When an accurate reading of winds is difficult because of these influences, you can use the movement of high-level and middle-level clouds as indicators of general wind direction.

Use of Pocket Barometer and Wind Direction

Back in 1877, John M. Gould, in a book entitled *How to Camp Out,* wrote this warning.

> Do not be in a hurry to spend money on new inventions. Every
> year there is put upon the market some patent knapsack,
> folding stove, cooking utensil, or camp trunk and cot combined;
> and there are always for sale patent knives, forks and spoons all
> in one, drinking cups, folding portfolios, and marvels of tools.
> Let them all alone.

Over 100 years later, Mr. Gould's words are perhaps more apt than when they were written. Nevertheless, the advent of rugged, light, and compact pocket altimeter-barometers may be of interest to campers who are gadget-minded and weather-conscious.

You need to be aware that substantial fluctuations in temperature and elevation can make accurate barometric-pressure readings difficult while you are on the move. Nevertheless, your attention to general trends in the atmospheric pressure, coupled with observation of wind direction, can make for fairly accurate forecasting. By using a pocket barometer while you are in a stationary position such as your camp, you can note whether the atmospheric pressure is steady, changing slowly, or changing rapidly.

The use of a pocket altimeter-barometer, like this one made by Thommen, coupled with observation of the wind direction, can make forecasting the general weather trends more accurate. PEET BROS. COMPANY, INC.

Term	*Change in barometric reading within 3 hours*
Steady	Less than 0.01″
Changing slowly	Between 0.01″ and 0.05″
Changing rapidly	More than 0.05″

Use these *trends* (not specific pressure readings) along with wind direction and the following table to predict rain with your morning granola or an upcoming day of cycling in the sun.

WIND-BAROMETER TABLE*

Wind direction	*Sea-level barometric pressure in inches*	*Character of weather indicated*
SW to NW	30.10 to 30.20 and steady	Fair, with little temperature change, for 1 to 2 days.
SW to NW	30.10 to 30.20 and rising rapidly	Fair, followed within 2 days by warmer and rain.
SW to NW	30.20 and above and stationary	Continued fair with no marked temperature change.
SW to NW	30.20 and above and falling slowly	Fair with slowly rising temperature for 2 days.
S to SE	30.10 to 30.20 and falling slowly	Rain within 24 hours.
S to SE	30.10 to 30.20 and falling rapidly	Wind increasing in force, with rain within 12 to 24 hours.
SE to NE	30.10 to 30.20 and falling slowly	Rain in 12 to 18 hours.

* U.S. Weather Bureau Table

Wind direction	Sea-level barometric pressure in inches	Character of weather indicated
SE to NE	30.10 to 30.20 and falling rapidly	Increasing wind and rain within 12 hours.
E to NE	30.10 and above and falling slowly	In summer, with light winds, rain may not fall for several days. In winter, rain within 24 hours.
E to NE	30.10 and above and falling rapidly	In summer, rain probably within 12 to 24 hours. In winter, rain or snow, with increasing winds.
SE to NE	30.00 or below and falling slowly	Rain will continue 1 to 2 days.
SE to NE	30.00 or below and falling rapidly	Rain with high winds, followed by clearing, and in winter by colder, within 36 hours.
S to SW	30.00 or below and rising slowly	Clearing within a few hours and fair for several days.
S to E	29.80 or below and falling rapidly	Severe storm soon, followed within 24 hours by clearing, and in winter by colder.
E to N	29.80 or below and falling rapidly	Severe northeast gale and heavy precipitation. In winter, heavy snow followed by a cold wave.
Going to W	29.80 or below and rising rapidly	Clearing and colder.

Both the sun and the moon have a daily influence on a barometer, so you should make some minor adjustments while taking your readings. In the U.S., your barometer will rise 0.04" between 5 and 9 (both a.m. and p.m., standard time) and will fall 0.04" between 11 and 3 (both a.m. and p.m.). Consequently, for each hour between 5 and 9 that you keep track of barometric pressure, subtract 0.01" from any trends you have noted. Add 0.01" for each hour you follow the barometer between 11 and 3. For example, if your barometer reads 30.02" at 5 o'clock when you stop to make camp and 30.06" at 9 o'clock, there has actually been no appreciable change in barometric pressure. If, on the other hand, your barometer is 30.00" at noon on an in-camp rest day and 30.03" at 3 o'clock, it is showing a rapid rise. It has actually changed 0.06" within three hours.

Weather Lore

While it's true that a barometer is a handy tool for measuring air pressure, the presence of an instrument like this is unnerving to many campers. In the wilds the dial, calibrations, and calculations all seem out of place, just as the presence of a transistor radio or T.V. would be. The trappings of a mechanized society seem somehow blasphemous in the silence of a conifer forest or the expanse of a Great Plains prairie. It needn't be mentioned that most of the gear we take with us into the backcountry is the product of a highly technological world. Still, many of us prefer to live with the illusion of simplicity and primitive self-sufficiency. Things like barometers can cloud the illusion.

How much better it is, in the minds of many campers, to use uncomplicated signs of nature that suggest at a glance what weather might be on the way. For centuries, Indians, explorers, and mountain men used smoke from their fires to predict weather. Smoke acts as a primitive barometer. When low pressure invades the area, smoke will not rise but will curl toward the ground. But in the good weather associated with high pressure, smoke rises and dissipates quickly.

Sailors used another sign, which is described by a rhyme familiar to many of us.

> Red sky at night, sailors delight,
> Red sky at morning, sailors take warning.

The saying has firm foundation in fact. A rising sun will color red any rain clouds forming in the western sky, the direction from which changes in weather will most likely come. If the clouds are past you and moving off to your east, the sun setting in the west will likewise turn those clouds red.

Rainbows act in a similar way to predict short-range weather changes. A morning sun shining through rain clouds to your west will create a rainbow. A rainbow is also caused by an evening sun hitting rain to your east, where it is already past you. Early founders of the wool industry must have been responsible for this observation:

> Rainbow in the morning, shepherds take warning;
> Rainbow at night, shepherd's delight.

Some campers who are addicted to sleeping out in the open under any conditions have developed another interesting method of forecasting weather. If they wake up in the morning and their sleeping bags are wet with dew (or covered with frost), the day will be fine. Dew (and frost) forms when objects on the ground cool below the condensation point (dew point) of the surrounding air. Since the greatest cooling by radiation occurs when the skies are clear, campers under the stars are right to believe that

> When the dew is on the grass,
> Rain will never come to pass.

Of course, if they wake up to find their sleeping bags covered with rain, this too indicates something about the weather. No one yet has created a rhyme for the phenomenon.

A Spanish proverb points out, though, that

> When God wills, it rains with any wind.

That's why, no matter how well you can read the skies or the rain on your sleeping bag, it's wise to know something about the clothes that can keep the rain off your back.

Dew on leaves or grass when you wake up in the morning is a good natural indicator of clear skies for that day.

2

Rain Clothes

From man's beginnings, water has been in the myths, songs, and legends of the world as a primal creator and sustainer of life. It has nurtured crops, animals, and the souls of men for as long as memory serves. And so it seems only fitting that each one of us was surrounded by water before our birth.

But somewhere in the process of maturing we seem to lose our close physical affinity with water. Children still like to go out and play bareheaded in the rain while stomping in puddles. Yet the older we get, the more we shrink from falling rain.

Perhaps that's why centuries have been spent in the search for the ideal waterproof material. Until recently nothing has approached perfection. Any material, like plastic or rubber, that can truly keep rain out, also holds body moisture in. As a result, the backpacker chugging up the trail in his rubberized parka doesn't feel a drop of the rain that's falling. But he starts to simmer in his own sweat and in the condensation that forms on the *inside* of his waterproof rainwear. If you're quietly crunching granola around camp, such garments are fine. When you start to leap tall buildings in a single bound, you get soaked from the skinside out.

Although our skin is quite waterproof, the adults of our species seem obsessed with putting on clothes that will help them stay dry.

The alternative to using clothing that is waterproof has traditionally been to use gear that is water-repellent. Materials of this type let the water vapor produced by your bodily gyrations escape to the outside air; for this reason, they are said to breathe. The problem is that water-repellent clothing will shed rain only so long. Eventually moisture is going to soak through to you. So until recently, the choice between waterproof and water-repellent clothing has been a damp-if-you-do, damp-if-you-don't proposition.

It seems that after centuries of searching, some waterproof and breathable materials have finally been made. Although they aren't miracle fabrics (they won't, for instance, prevent you from working up a good sweat), they do keep out rain and they do permit the escape of water vapor. These new materials don't make all other fabrics obsolete, but they do add a very refreshing new dimension to the possible kinds of rainwear.

Materials

A number of natural and synthetic materials are used for wet-weather clothing. Each has its advantages and disadvantages.

Nylon

Of all the materials used in rain gear, nylon is the strongest for its weight. It is also highly resistant to rot and mildew. It therefore has a definite place in the realm of mist and moisture. Because nylon strands are solid and won't absorb moisture, the material dries quickly. However, it doesn't hold a water-repellent treatment very well, and it will feel clammy to the touch in humid or rainy weather. I can report from first-hand discomfort that a nylon wind shirt worn next to the skin feels like the slither of a wet snake. For this reason, pure nylon garments that are unlined with an absorbent material are better left for outer wear.

Weathering, especially at high elevations in strong sunlight, is the primary cause for nylon's loss in strength, which is one more good reason to hike with gladness on those dim, dark days.

Dacron

Although Dacron isn't as strong as nylon, neither is it as elastic. So Dacron lends itself to a much tighter weave than nylon. This quality could mean a decrease in the invasion of outside moisture.

Orlon

Orlon is not as strong as other synthetics yet is highly resistant to deterioration caused by weather. In addition, when spun into yarn and used in clothing, Orlon has many of the characteristics of wool but it stronger than wool, especially when wet.

Polyester

Once found only in "leisure suits" and often the butt of social class jokes, polyester took the outdoor clothing market by storm in the 1980s. The basic synthetic fiber has gone through numerous refinements. It's been made thinner (it's now called a "micro-fiber"); it's been coated with various substances to help it shed and wick moisture, and it's been woven and "brushed" in different ways to make it more windproof, tear-resistant, and comfortable against the skin. You'll find it in everything from underwear to winter parkas, but its greatest contribution to our outdoor comfort comes in the form of pile clothing, which is very warm.

Polypropylene

"Polypro," as it's been dubbed, is the lightest and least absorbent synthetic fiber. Like polyester, it has become standard in outdoor clothing. Yet, it is probably best suited (at this stage in its development) for underwear.

Plastic and Rubber

Rubber and plastic, and fabrics that have been treated with plastic or rubber compounds, have traditionally been used in making waterproof clothing.

Plastic has the advantage of being light and inexpensive. I became intimately familiar with this material in the form of a cheap rainsuit that self-destructed upon apparent contact with ethereal spirits.

Plastic is better left untouched.

Rubber is heavier, more expensive, and more durable. It's found in the foul-weather gear designed for lobstermen who are intent on riding out nor'easters.

Both rubber and plastic have the habit of keeping rain out and sweat in.

Cotton

Because cotton fibers have little stretch, they can be woven into a very tight fabric. The fibers are also absorbent and will swell when wet, making a tightly woven garment almost waterproof while still breathable. Cotton's absorbent quality makes it easily treated with water-repellent compounds, whether done commercially or at home. However, cotton isn't as strong as synthetics; it takes a long time to dry, and it shrinks easily. It is also susceptible to mildew and rotting. Finally, wet cotton is cold and provides no insulation. If you've ever slogged around in soaked blue jeans, you know the feeling.

Wool

Wool is extremely effective in wet weather and is a favorite of Maine guides as well as Western wranglers. Soft and bulky, it retains much of its insulating value when wet because moisture doesn't mat down its fibers. Also, with the help of body heat, wool tends to dry from within and works to draw moisture away from your body. An oiled-wool sweater (one that has been treated with natural lanolin) is surprisingly water-repellent, even though it develops its own distinctive aroma. Although wool isn't very strong and will both shrink and stretch, it should be a permanent part of your wet-weather wardrobe.

Blends

In an attempt to combine the positive qualities of two materials, several blended fabrics have been created. Probably best known is 60/40 cloth, which has become so common in mountain parkas. This is a blend of 60% cotton and 40% nylon. The cotton threads run in one direction of the weave, and nylon threads run at right angles to the cotton. The cotton swells in the rain to make a tight material, and it allows the garment to hold a water-repellent treatment. The nylon adds strength, resists abrasion, and reduces weight.

More and more frequently, 65/35 cloth is appearing in outdoor clothing. It is cotton/Dacron polyester combined in an intimate blend. In other words, fibers of the two materials are combined in the thread before the fabric is woven. Proponents of 65/35 cloth claim it is stronger than 60/40 cloth and accepts water-repellents more readily.

Other cotton/polyester blends include 50/50 cloth and even one called 83/17 cloth. How's that for splitting hairs? At the time of this writing, however, 60/40 parkas and their variants are getting hard to find. Modern technology may soon make them as rare as grizzly bears in the lower 48 states.

Breathable Waterproofs

Gore-Tex® was the first so-called "breathable" waterproof. It came on the outdoor scene in 1976 after first being used in medical procedures as a replacement for human tissue. In clothing, a thin Gore-Tex membrane is used between two and three layer laminates, usually of nylon or nylon taffeta. The membrane is made of the catchy hi-tech stuff called polytetrafluoroethylene, PTFE for short. It's a form of Teflon® that has been stretched thin enough to have 9 billion pores per square inch. I have not counted them. But each pore is 20,000 times smaller than a drop of water, yet 700 times larger than a molecule of water vapor! These guys are good with their tape measures.

Now, according to the United States Army, a material is waterproof when it will withhold water pressure of 25 pounds per square inch (psi). "But," say W. L. Gore and Associates, "the pressure of wind-driven rain, or the pressure from just kneeling and sitting on wet surfaces, can be as high as 25 psi." Gore-Tex, they claim, will withstand water pressure to a minimum of 60 psi (and some versions up to 150 psi) before water will leak through the material. Yet it will let water *vapor* escape through it about as well as a tightly woven cotton garment.

There were two major complaints about "first generation" Gore-Tex. The first was that garments made with the film leaked at the seams unless they were coated with two generous coats of liquid seam sealer. The second complaint was that Gore-Tex leaked after it came in contact with body oils and sweat. So, in 1978, "second generation" Gore-Tex hit the

Parkas made of material that is both waterproof and breathable offer the best protection against rain and condensation.

market with factory sealed seams and with an oil repellent impregnated into the PTFE. Both new procedures were designed to solve the initial leakage problems. Gore-Tex took off in sales and has stayed on top of the breathable waterproof market ever since.

But other breathable waterproofs have gotten into the outdoor garment act in the last decade. There are laminates like Sympatex® and Thintech®. And there are microporous coatings like Entrant®, H2NO Plus®, Helly-Tech®, and Ultrex®. Sierra Design has just come out with a breathable waterproof called Hokus Pokus®. Hind has Freeflex® in a tight-fitting running suit. All of them have their own claims for keeping you dry while the world around you is wet, but much of an outer garment's weather-worthiness is as much in its design and construction as it is in the materials it's made of.

Water-Repellents and Waterproof Coatings

Many of the materials already mentioned, especially the synthetics and the blends, must be treated commercially or at home to produce and maintain their water-repellent or waterproof qualities.

Water-Repellents

Most tight-weave water-repellent garments are factory treated with something like DuPont Zepel, which will wear out in time. Sunlight and dirt are the greatest enemies of this kind of finish. You can reduce the harmful effects of sunlight by camping in the rain. In addition, you can try to keep your rain gear clean. If you take it to a dry cleaner, require them to use a pure dry-cleaning solvent. At home, if you aren't totally inept, you can effectively use something like Pure Stoddard's solvent to clean your parka, or you can wash it in warm water with a mild soap, not a detergent. Either way, giving it an ironing after a washing or cleaning will help renew its water repellency. Don't have the iron too hot or it will melt materials like nylon.

When you find it necessary to recoat a garment with a water-repellent compound, a dry cleaner can do the job. You can also do it yourself with something like Scotchgard, Rain-Dri, or Gard, all of which will probably have a silicone base.

Waterproofs

Waterproofing treatments are most successfully applied during the manufacture of the material or the garment. Nevertheless, urethane coatings like those sold by Kenyon (Super K-Kote, Heat Sealable K-Kote, and so on) can be used at home. But it's possible that these do-it-yourself treatments may decrease the tear strength of the material and peal or crack in cold weather. Few things are worse than a rain parka that has the heartbreak of psoriasis.

Rain Clothes

There is a wide variety in the design and construction of rainwear. Some items won't keep you dry in a sneeze. Others may be fine for hikers but impossible for bikers. When you select rain clothes, think about your needs carefully. Consider what kind of rain protection you're looking for, and examine the specific features of each item. But whatever you buy, make sure it is large enough to go over other layers of clothing without being tight.

The matter of rainwear design shouldn't be taken lightly. W. L. Gore, the maker of Gore-Tex, certainly doesn't. For years after "second generation" Gore-Tex came on the market, they were still getting complaints that Gore-Tex garments were leaking. But their own tests of the garments that were getting people wet showed that, in most cases, the problem was not in the fabric but in the design and construction of the clothing.

So, in 1989, W. L. Gore started a licensing program called Partners in Performance. In essence, it means that they will only deal with clothing manufacturers who are willing to sign a licensing agreement to "meet certain standards for waterproofness and breathability along with functional and aesthetic characteristics" in their Gore-Tex clothing.

Under this agreement, each garment design is tested in a special rain chamber approved by Gore. "The Rain Test" simulates conditions equivalent to three inches of rain falling in an hour. Garments that pass this test get a "Guaranteed to Keep You Dry" hang tag. "The Storm Test" blasts garments with the equivalent of twenty-two inches of rain per hour, and if it survives without leaking, that item of rainwear gets the "Guaranteed to Keep You Dry" tag with "For Extreme Wet Weather" added.

Now, I am not on the payroll of W. L. Gore, but I am impressed with their guarantee. I've talked with the people at Gore, and they have assured me that they will test any Gore-Tex garment that is suspected of being leaky and will replace it, at no cost, if it fails their test.

What that says to you and me is this: we may not be able to look at a specific item of rainwear and determine that it has been properly sealed at the seams, or that it has been constructed with "gutter flaps" or with "moisture dams," but the "Guaranteed to Keep You Dry" tag indicates that the damn thing *ought* to keep you dry. And that, after all, is the only reason you should be willing to spend lots of money on a breathable waterproof garment in the first place. So endeth the unsolicited pitch for Gore-Tex.

Parka

Many campers associate a parka with the currently popular "mountain parka" or "60/40 parka," which is named for the material it's made of. Typically, these parkas have a full-length zipper opening down the front, making them easy to put on and take off. They are finger-tip length and have a hood and large pockets. Beyond these standard features, the designs vary.

One of the most important aspects of a rain parka is its hood. A hood that doesn't turn with your head is particularly annoying when your hands are full of handle-bars or paddle. Look for a recessed drawstring and a contoured hood. Both will help your hood and head turn together. To make sure they do, I usually wear a billed baseball type hat under my parka hood in all but extremely cold weather. In addition, a hood with a stiffened visor or bill will help keep rain off your face and glasses. And a hood that can be rolled up and fastened under tabs won't collect water when you want just a hat on your head.

I once watched a disgruntled cyclist battening down his hatches in the face of an increasing rain. During the preceding light-but-steady precipitation, his loose hood had caught perhaps half a cup of water.

From the look on the unfortunate fellow's face, that half cup must have felt like a cold gallon as it coursed down his neck and around his midriff.

Another thing to look for in a good parka is adjustable ventilation. Even when the garment is made of a breathable material, you'll want air circulation when you're on the trail, unless it's extremely windy or cold. Look for adjustable wrist and waist closures. If they're made of elastic, heat will always be closed in at these points. You'll end up sweating more than you have to. Some parkas have zippered vent openings under their armpits; these can be effective in keeping you cool while the rest of you is kept dry.

The workmanship in a garment is important. Check the seams for neatness and number of stitches. Crooked stitching is not what you want to buy. Six to twelve stitches per inch is a good standard. Any more or less can cause weaknesses. In rain gear, double seams or heat-sealed seams are the most effective. But be especially wary of any seams at the shoulders, where they are highly vulnerable to leakage.

When it comes to materials, many mountain and 60/40 parkas are intended more for protection against wind that against rain. The 60/40 cloth and even 65/35 cloth just can't be woven tightly enough to be highly water-repellent, so they will soak through in a prolonged rain. These materials are particularly susceptible to soaking through where rubbing occurs, such as under shoulder straps when you're backpacking. In an attempt to avoid this problem, a variation has been tried.

Performance Bike Shop, 800-PBS-BIKE
This parka by Performance has a fold-down tail for spray protection.

The 60/40 parka is made of a waterproofed nylon material for its hood, shoulders and sleeves. The rest of the garment is made of a breathable polyester/cotton blend. The design was originated by Jan Sport.

Breathable waterproof parkas have become extremely popular, and they come in a wide variety of designs. A new line of cycling parkas is put out by Performance They've designed one parka (which comes with pants) with a fold-down tail for spray protection. This parka has a drawstring at the waist, elastic wrist closures, and a detachable hood.

Rain Jacket

A rain jacket is usually hip length and may or may not have a hood. This garment most commonly is made of cheap, light, transparent plastic or heavy and fairly expensive rubberized materials. The plastic versions may last you one trip, but at their low prices most people can afford it. The rubberized models give you longer-lasting wear but are too heavy and bulky for all but a canoe or raft trip. Both types of jacket will parboil you on all but a winter trip, so they're of rather limited usefulness for hikers and bikers.

Anorak

In contemporary usage, the term anorak refers to a parka-like garment that has no zipper going all the way down the front. It might have a short zipper at the neck, but this is usually no more than six inches long. The idea is that a zipper might break or leak or otherwise cause problems in really nasty weather. Of course you look and feel like an octopus that's attempting headstands while you're putting on or taking off an anorak, particularly when you are already wearing several layers of clothes.

All the features that would enhance a parka do the same for an anorak. When all is said and done, however, you're still left with one big drawback: an anorak can't be opened up in the front, so adjusting the ventilation is restricted. In any kind of rain, whether hot or cold, this limitation puts you at a considerable disadvantage.

Cagoule

A cagoule (it sounds like something that should be used to keep rain off a gargoyle) is a calf-length anorak that is cut very fully. The design was originated for mountain climbers who might be forced to bivouac—that is, to camp without a shelter—usually between a rock and a hard place.

A cagoule is usually waterproofed and is long and full enough to allow you to pull your legs up inside when you're sitting or lying down. Then the bottom can be sealed off against the weather with the drawstring at the hem. More stretched-out protections can be provided by sticking your legs into a pack and cinching the bottom of the cagoule around it.

Either way, you'd find this rather like trying to get comfortable in the confines of a burlap bag. Hikers and cyclists will find a cagoule too restricting on the trail. Canoeists may find it useful, but the nagging matter of condensation is still there, except in Gore-Tex models. For all practical purposes, a cagoule is only useful as in-camp rainwear.

Poncho

The poncho is probably the most popular rain garment for hikers. Basically, it's a sheet of material ranging from 4' x 7' to 5' x 10' and having a head hole with a hood situated approximately in its center. The larger models are designed to go over both you and your pack. A poncho is a sort of well-vented cross between a parka and a cagoule, and it can run from a cheap plastic version to a coated nylon model. Also, there are still some heavy rubberized Army-surplus types lying around discount stores.

A good poncho will have fasteners and grommets along its edges. The fasteners, when snapped together, will form baggy sleeves. Because this outfit fits loosely, it provides good ventilation. But where heat and moisture can escape, rain can enter. In a windy rain, your poncho may billow like a parachute, letting rain in from various directions.

Some ponchos have internal ties at the waist to keep them in place. You can also put a belt or some string around the outside to hold them down. In either case, closing off the waist will tend to make you heat up and drip in warm weather. One perpetual annoyance is the problem of water dripping off your poncho hem onto your pants. If it's warm, you can wear shorts and let the drips fall on your skin. You can wear rain pants or chaps (see page 29). Or you can try the inexpensive trip of rubbing wax on your pants to waterproof them at the points where the drips land. This usually ends up being a walk-walk-was, walk-walk-wax routine.

Despite the obvious drawbacks of a poncho, it will serve the backpacker as a benevolent billowing refuge in all but prolonged, heavy rain, or at high elevations where extreme wind, rain, cold, and even snow may be likely. It is probably the least expensive of rain garments, and it has an added advantage: it can be rigged to provide a variety of shelters from rain, wind, and sun.

Although any poncho is a bit too voluminous for the movements of a canoeist, there is a special cycling poncho. This is specifically cut to fit the

A poncho is an extremely versatile garment for protecting you and your gear, and it can be made into various shelters.

contours of your body while you're perched on your seat, peddling. It has hand and leg loops, which help to keep the garment in place while you're moving. But it may lead to an unexpected try at hang gliding.

Pants

Pants have always been a problem in wet weather. Jeans are cold and clammy when wet. And although Cabela's has just come out with Gore-Tex blue jeans, I look down at the holey jeans I'm writing in and wonder a lot about that combination. Wool, which repels water fairly well and is still comfortable when wet, is too hot for many situations. When the weather is warm and you don't need protection against brush or other spiny vegetation, you can travel in shorts and expose your legs. It's often better to do this so you can save your dry long pants for camp. Plowing through scrub oak or creosotebush, on the other hand, can turn legs into steak tartare. Filson makes long pants, appropriately called "tin" pants, for this kind of thrashing about. They are made of heavy-duty 10-ounce water-repellent duck and will take a great deal of flagellation. In either long or short pants, a cotton/polyester blend corduroy, such as that put out by Woolrich, is fairly water-repellent. In heavy rain, however, even these will get wet.

For those storms that are real toad stranglers, rain pants or rain chaps worn over your regular shorts or long pants are the only answer. These come in the traditional waterproofed materials plus the newer breathable waterproofs. The chaps are best for hikers and canoeists because they provide ventilation at the crotch. Bikers are stuck with wearing rain pants because of the considerable amount of spray that comes from beneath.

Clothes for Women

A number of years ago, Sarah Rahaim created a design for shorts and pants just for women. The garments have a Velcro vent on the inner leg seam, which can be opened for quick relief when nature calls. I'm told that underpants are no problem and can just be pulled to one side. Besides having this fast-relief feature, these clothes—called QP shorts and pants—are especially cut for women's shapes. They are made of 65/35 cloth and may be just the thing for a QP in a cloudburst. I've been unable to confirm whether Sarah's designs are still available in 1991.

However, the long-standing problem women have had in getting outdoor clothing that fits well is finally beginning to ease. More and more manufacturers are offering clothes in ladies' sizes and cuts. May the trend continue.

Shirts and Sweaters for All Hands

For wet-weather items, wool is an effective material. It is the traditional material for bicycling jerseys. For hikers and canoeists, a very light wool shirt or pullover may be tolerable e ven in fairly warm weather. A wool sweater will add more warmth when it's needed. However, when temperatures get too warm for wool, almost any comfortable shirt will do under outer rain gear, but keep in mind the pros and cons of the various materials.

Polyester pile has really come into its own. Most new pile doesn't pill the way the old stuff did. It's very soft and it doesn't feel clammy next to your skin. A light pile pullover makes an excellent shirt for the rain.

Underwear

Nylon-and-wool or medium-weight polypropylene blends in fish-net underwear were by far the best things to wear next to the skin when I first wrote this book in 1980. Fish-net ventilates extremely well under loose clothing because air can circulate through the weave. It also insulates effectively under close-fitting clothes like turtlenecks. In the past, only long fish-net underpants were available. Now, short fish-net underpants are available for use in warm weather. Bikers may find that seams and even the net in this type of underpants leave intricate and tender patterns indelibly engraved in their skin after sitting on a narrow bicycle seat all day. Backpackers, when selecting a net undershirt, should be sure to get one with soft-knit shoulders so that chafing won't occur where pack straps hit.

A refined version of the original fishnet unders (shirt only) is being offered by Recreational Equipment, Inc., in their 1991 catalog. Called the Sonora T-shirt, this polyester version is described, in the hi-tech catalog jargon of most mail-order shopping places of the

'90s, as being made of APT (Accelerated Perspiration Transport) fabric.

Behind the jargon of APT is the essence of why polyester and polypro underwear has become so popular. The synthetic fibers, in their various new forms, draw moisture away from the skin and into outer layers of clothing, where it both dissipates into the air and is dried by body heat. You don't get that cold, clammy feeling after you've worked up a sweat and evaporative cooling sets in.

Hats

You're best rainy-day head protection is under the hood attached to your rain shell. If you find that the tunnel vision offered by a hood is too restricting, or that a hood is too hot, or that the rain is light, a tight-weaver wool, felt, or coated-nylon hat will keep most of the rain off your pate. Pile and other polyester hats now come in many soft varieties and are ideal because of their moisture-shedding virtues. My experience with cotton hats is that they shrink with the first good soaking and, thereafter, make you feel as if your head has swollen.

Keeping moisture off your neck requires a wide brim. This is no problem for canoeists. But backpackers will find that a substantial brim is constantly colliding with the packframe and that certain pruning may be in order. Cyclists will immediately lose or discard a wide-brimmed hat and go back to a well-tied-down hood as the only reasonable headgear to wear in the rain.

Footwear

Hiking, biking, and canoeing each pose special and different problems in protecting your feet against water. It's not only the falling rain you must worry about. The rain forms troublesome lakes on the trail and in the bottom of your canoe. Spray shoots up against bikers from streams that form on the road.

Hiking Boots

Except in espcially soggy places, traditional leather hiking boots are
perfectly serviceable for the backpacker. Leather boots, when properly
treated, are surprisingly water repellent. Full-grain leather (the outside
surface of the cow after the hair has been removed) is the most water-
repellent. And boots with uppers made of one piece of leather are less apt to
lead, because they have only one seam. Make sure seams are sewn with a
synthetic thread like nylon or Dacron. Cotton thread will rot almost before
you get out of your first puddle. Although much has been written about
different types of welt (the way in which the upper of the boot is attached to
the sold), the details of this aspect of boot construction aren't as important to
water resistance as some folks claim.

The most important concern in keeping boots water-resistant is the
way you treat them. When you buy a boot, be sure you find out how
the leather was tanned. If the boot was chrome-tanned, it should be
treated with a wax-based or silicone-based compound like Sno-Seal.
An oil-tanned boot should have an oil-based treatment such as
Huberd's Shoe Grease. These water-repellents should only be used
on the uppers, since they can weaken the cement and stitching when
put on the welt. The welt area should be treated with something like
Stitch Lock or Leath-R-Seal.

Some special wet-hiking situations may call for specialized footwear. In
some parts of the country, boots have even been designed to cope with the
local wet conditions. Although the L.L. Bean Maine Hunting Shoe is not the
best boot for long-range backpacking, it is made to match the soggy
backcountry conditions of its native and surrounding states. The boot has
rubber bottoms that extend to just below the ankle. The uppers are of full-
grain leather. With this arrangement, the lower part of your boot can be in
water constantly without your feet getting wet, and the leather uppers still
let your feet breathe. An all-rubber boot would be hot and sweaty in all but
cold weather, and an all-leather boot would eventually soak through under
marshy conditions.

Some of the most unusual and fascinating trips in the Southwest
require hiking in canyons that are still being carved by the rivers that
flow through them. In places like the Paria Canyon, the Virgin River
"Narrows," and the Escalante River country, the only place for a trail
is in the river bottom. Some hikers wear sneakers for such a trip. But

sneakers offer little support and provide poor protection for the soles of your feet. Besides, they easily fill with sand and pebbles. For such really wet backpacking, I'd recommend G.I. tropical combat boots. The bottom part of the upper is leather; the top part is a nylon/cotton canvas. The boot has lugged soles and grommetlike vent/drainage holes at the arch. These tropical combat boots are light and offer support. And, water, once it gets in, has a convenient means of escape.

In the 1980s, some of the running shoe makers got into the hiking boot business. The results are fabric boots, reinforced with leather, that look like composites of traditional hiking boots, tropical combat boots, and modern running shoes. They have their virtues (light weight, fast-drying, no break-in) and some drawbacks (difficult to waterproof and lack of foot/ankle support under heavy loads). But they are definitely here to stay, and they will show up frequently in wet places even if they're not on your feet.

Gore-Tex has also worked its way into both leather and fabric hiking boots. And I must say that my original misgivings have been put to rest after several years of using a pair of Danner leather/Gore-Tex boots in many kinds of wet. "They do keep my feet dry!" I say with surprise.

In boggy country, a rubber-bottom, leather-top boot, like the L.L. Bean Hunting Shoe, helps keep your feet dry while still allowing them to breathe.

Performance Bike Shop, 800-PBS-BIKE

Neoprene shoe covers will keep feet warm and dry.

Biking Boots

The only way to have dry feet when biking in the rain is to wear a pair of waterproof booties over your cycling shoes. Combined with a pair of rain pants, these booties will keep your lower extremities protected from outside moisture. Neoprene bike shoe covers are on the market. You'll also find Gore-Tex in both bike shoes and bike shoe covers. Yes, folks, it's everywhere, it's everywhere. In a real pinch, plastic bags worn over your shoes, or over your feet inside your shoes, will protect you for a little while.

Canoe Shoes

Low-cut sneakers are common footwear for canoeing. They're light, they have good traction on canoe bottoms, and they dry out quickly. Also available is Uniroyal's fast-drying canoe shoe, which is made of polyester mesh. When you're in the middle of a real duck drencher, you can always tuck your feet under the canoe seat for proection. Of course, the bottom of a canoe can get kind of sloppy in a downpour. But by the time your feet are in danger of getting soaked, you should have thought about bailing. For a bit more protection from bilge water, however, you may want to consider something like L.L. Bean's rubber moccasins.

Socks

Socks, especially for hikers, can do a lot more than many folks think. They can act as shock absorbers for the feet; they can reduce friction between foot and boot; they can help keep your feet warm or cool; and, most important when it's damp, they can help keep your feet dry.

Before you ever buy a pair of hiking boots, you've got to decide what kind of socks or combination of socks you'll want to wear with them, otherwise you won't get a proper fit. If you are going to wear only one pair of socks, a good choice would be a heavy pair made of 100% wool, or 85% wool with 15% nylon to reinforce toe and heel. Another good choice is a pair of "wick" socks of 50% orlon, 40% nylon, and 10% cotton. The nonabsorbent inner layer wicks moisture to the absorbent outer layer and keeps your feet fairly dry. These socks can be worn when you're more concerned with keeping your feet dry than with keeping them warm.

When I'm hiking in wet weather, I prefer wearing a combination of two pairs of socks. A lightweight inner sock of polypropylene is nonabsorbent, long-lasting, and very efficient in transmitting moisture to the outer sock. The outer socks I use are medium-to-heavy wool. There are socks available that have a inner layer of polypropylene and an outer layer of wool for those folks who prefer to wear only one pair of socks. I find these good for canoeing and bicycling.

Gaiters

Socks and boots are sometimes not enough to offer suitable protection from moisture. Wet grass and brush can soak you from the knees down nearly as fast as a wade in a lake. Gaiters are the things to use in these situations. Made of coated nylon or Gore-Tex, these waterproof sleeves fit over the tops of your boots and extend up your legs. Both ends are elasticized; the bottom has a strap to go below your instep, and the side often has a full-length zipper to facilitate putting the gaiter on and taking it off. Gaiters come in varying heights. I prefer the knee length.

Knee-length gaiters will protect your lower legs against wet vegetation and offer some protection to your hiking boots.

That completes the wet-weather wardrobe. It has its subtleties, but some of the items may already be hanging in your closet or stuffed into a drawer. Don't think that because you lack the latest thing in rainwear you should sit home when a little moisture threatens. I can remember a time as a teenager when my sister and I tramped the Presidential Range in New Hampshire with no specially purchased clothing except hooded rain parkas. We squished up and down the humps of the presidents in a misty rain that seemed only fitting for our last night's stop at Lake of the Clouds hut. Despite the weather and our low-budget rain gear, we had a splendid time, especially with the people we met at the huts. I've remembered that rain-enshrouded trip fondly over the years. But in the intervening time, I've also learned that there's more to staying comfortable in wet weather than just wet-weather clothing.

3

Living in the Rain

Making life comfortable for yourself when you're out in rain and such requires a positive frame of mind as well as proper clothing, equipment, and techniques. Standing around doing nothing but grousing about the weather is a sure way to bring on a severe case of melancholia.

Besides, rain is responsible for enhancing many aspects of the surroundings through which you'll be moving. It brings out the earthy smell of moldering leaves in a Vermont forest and accentuates the aroma of pine along a Minnesota canoe trail. A fine mist can soften the outline of the Texas hill country or brighten the red lichen on a Wyoming granite slab. Rain festoons vine maples with moss in the Cascades; in the Smokies, it enlivens a rotting log with innumerable mushrooms. Many of the natural occurrences you see, smell, and touch owe their unique flavor to just plain rain.

Savoring this natural evidence of the rain's influence can keep you attentive to its positive aspects. But sometimes you have to get involved with other activities to help you forget about the rain's unpleasant sides—the soggy boots and the clammy toilet paper for example. That principle was once again reinforced on a hike I took not long ago with my wife and nephew. We'd spent the first night at Avalanche Lake, which, to judge from the surrounding terrain, seemed appropriately named. Here we fished for cutthroat trout amidst blustery winds that seemed to be pushing a front in our direction. The next day dawned grey as a water ouzel's breast.

But we were intent on tasting the fish in neighboring Blue Danube Lake, so down came the tent and off we went. By lunch time we had camp reestablished in the mouth of a wailing wind and spitting rain. The cutthroat weren't interested in a thing we cast so our interests turned back to camp, where the rest of the afternoon seemed to stretch out long and wet.

I guess it took half an hour of quiet and collective brooding before Linda recognized the futility of our gloomy moods. She announced her intention of spending the afternoon in the tent with a novel. Being novelless, I suggested to Mark that we take a wet-weather tour of the lakeshore; whereupon the afternoon brightened for all of us, and the rain disappeared from inside our heads if not from outside our parka hoods. Mark and I rock-hopped and glissaded in patches of snow; we marveled at the cracked halves of a house-size boulder, split, no doubt, by the forces of freezing water. We even laughed at the irony of seeing sunshine far below in the valley from which we'd come. Dinner that night was a happy, chatty occasion punctured by the hiss of rain on hot coals. At the end of that agreeably damp day, we knew we'd sleep well to the tune of raindrops on the roof.

Your mental attitude cannot, of course, work miracles. A cyclist without rain pants in a cool rain is going to be uncomfortable no matter how great are his powers of positive thinking. And the wet-weather hiker who doesn't know how to choose a suitable campsite may enjoy the tart smell of huckleberries along a damp mountain hillside, but he won't like the sensation of water in his bed. In the end, proper gear and techniques both on the trail and in camp must be your first defenses against harsh weather.

Canoe Trails

Canoeing in the rain when you're protected by good rain clothes can be quite comfortable if the temperature doesn't drop too low. What the wet-weather canoeist must be most wary of is the wind that often accompanies the moisture. Even on relatively small bodies of water, a summer squall can kick up dangerous waves. If you happen to be out in the middle of a lake when the wind hits, the only choice you may have is to turn your stern to the wind and head for shore, even if it's not the direction you want to go. So whenever you expect rain to be blowing in, it's wise to stay close to shore. A swamped canoe is not the ideal way to keep yourself and your gear dry.

Old Town Canoe

When squalls are likely, canoeists are well advised to head for shore to sit out the storm.

Recreational Equipment, Inc.

These modern versions of "black bags" will keep your gear dry while you are canoeing.

Canoe Luggage

Any kind of pack or container you use on a canoe trip should either be waterproof or have a waterproof cover. The cover may be only a tarp tied over your equipment. In that case, you should make floor boards, using 4 or 5 dead wood poles, to keep your gear off the bottom of the canoe where rain water will collect. A large sponge and can for bailing should be included to take care of any significant accumulation of water.

Custom-made spray-rain covers, which deck-in the entire canoe and have spray skirts over the seats, are available from both Grumman and Old Town Canoe companies. The Grumman cover fits all double-end 17-foot canoes and is attached with a stainless-steel cable and a tension device. Old Town has covers that fasten on with snaps and fit most of their open canoe models. These spray covers are expensive ($125 to $350), but are worth having if you plan to canoe extensively in wet weather.

Old Town Canoe

A canoe spray cover is worth having in whitewater.

• *Black Bags*—For the money, a black bag is still one of the best ways to go. These rubberized Army-surplus packs can still be found in many Army/Navy stores. They come in a variety of sizes and are very reasonably priced. The one I have has the capacity of a regular framepack and cost $5. Best of all, it really does keep things dry. I have gone into the water a few times with mine and afterwards have had dry clothes and a dry sleeping bag to console me.

Recreational Equipment, Inc., has lightweight versions of the old black bag. They are made of heavy-duty PVC-coated Dacron polyester. Sizes range from 13 x 16 x 32 inches to ditty bags of 10 x 17 inches.

• *Ammo Boxes*—Another Army-surplus deal is ammunition boxes. They will keep things dry if you make sure you get them with functional gaskets around the rims. They come in a variety of sizes. Although they do have carrying handles, they're awkward to portage any distance unless you can lash them to a packframe.

• *Boxes and Bags*—A number of other canoe boxes and bags are on the market at a variety of prices. When considering any of them, your main concerns should be that they are truly waterproof with a reliable closure system and that they are sturdy enough to resist punctures or cracks. Also choose containers that are easy to carry, if portaging plays a large part on your canoe trips.

Bike Trails

No other self-propelled traveler is faced with more problems from rain than is the cyclist. Rain comes down; it comes up; it is blown sideways, and it is recycled in the splashes of passing traffic. All-encompassing waterproof clothing is a must for a cyclist in a real downpour. But a few other things are also helpful.

Wet-Weather Bicycle Gear

• *Fenders and Mud Flaps*—That dingy strip that runs up your front and down your back can be partially avoided by the use of fenders and mud flaps. Although some cyclists find them just another annoying accessory that will inevitably need repair, anyone planning a long tour in the rain will be thankful to have them. The thing to look for in fenders is that they must not interfere with the placement or attachment of front and rear panniers or bags.

• *Packs and Panniers*—Your cycling luggage, particularly panniers that are mounted over the tries, are quite vulnerable to moisture. Although these items are usually made of coated nylon pack cloth, they can develop leaks. It's a good idea to add your own waterproofing to the cloth periodically. Also make sure that any carrier you buy has generous weather flaps over the zippers.

Performance Bike Shope, 800-PBS-BIKE

Since your cycling luggage will be subjected to moisture from above and beneath, packs and panniers should be well treated with waterproofing.

Cycling in the Rain

Since rain decreases your visibility and tends to make you lower your head into the wind, it is especially important to concentrate on what's happening around you. While your visibility is being impaired, something similar is happening to motorists approaching you. Put on your brightest-colored rain gear, and stay far over on the shoulder of the road.

Road surfaces can cause additional hazards. Many smooth-surface roads are oily and get very slippery when wet. Fallen leaves can make matters even worse. Puddles pose another problem. The spray from a passing automobile can hit with the force of a firehose, knocking you off balance and momentarily blinding you. Puddles can also conceal potholes and other dangers. A friend of mine once cycled into a puddle that covered some railroad tracks. The handlebars were wrenched from his grip, and ligaments were pulled in his knee. He and his bike completed the trip in a bus. Rainy-weather bicycling has to be defensive cycling.

Finally, the combination of moisture and the wind caused by your own movement can be extremely dangerous because of the wind and water chill factors (see Hypothermia, Chapter 4). Wear warm clothes under your rain gear.

Foot Trails

Wet Under Foot

You wouldn't think that a wet trail would cause too many problems for a hiker, but experience proves otherwise. Poorly constructed trails and those that get little maintenance (there are a lot in both categories) present mud, clay, and ooze as common problems. Wet roots and rocks are also treacherous. Sometimes a lake or stream develops where the trail once was.

All of these obstacles call for very careful footing. More often, they seem to encourage detours onto the drier more secure ground alongside the original trail. Unfortunately, repeated use of these detours causes further erosion. Eventually, two or three muddy troughs swing back and forth across one another. So when the footing isn't too treacherous, try to stay on the main trail. If traveling such a route means slipping and sliding at every step, however, a detour may be the only way to avoid a sprained ankle. In this case, make your detour well off the trail, where it's unlikely that other hikers will duplicate your footsteps.

Off-trail travel poses additional problems. Downed timber and rocks can be very slippery and should be avoided when possible. Wet vegetation, particularly on steep slopes, is another hazard. Soggy leaves, called "Tennessee Snow" in the Cumberland Mountains, require special attention.

In many areas, even where trails exist, bridges aren't provided for

Muddy trails often force hikers off to the side of the path. Sometimes rocks and logs along the edges can serve as stepping stones. But when lengthy detours are called for, make them well off the original trail in order to prevent further erosion.

stream or river crossings. This lack can cause wet "weather" conditions localized around your feet and legs, even when the sun's out.

When bridges, logs, and rocks don't cooperate and you must walk through water, you have a choice of four ways.

• First, you can simply walk in and wade across, making sure you unbuckle your pack's waist belt so you can jettison your load if you fall. This method makes for easy river crossing because your feet are protected. However, if also makes for uncomfortable, squishy walking later, and your wet socks can lead to blisters.

• Second, you can put boots and socks in your pack and wade across barefooted. I've tried it in water that was so cold I couldn't feel my feet. The result was a lacerated heel, caused, I assume, by wedging my foot between two rocks. But it was a pleasure to walk in dry boots and socks afterward.

• A third way is to take off your socks and put on just your boots. This compromise provides foot protection while you're crossing. Once across, you empty the boots and put back on the dry socks. The socks will still get wet, of course, but not as wet as they would if you wore them while wading.

• Finally, there's the method I've settled on whenever frequent crossings are probable. I carry a pair of sneakers in my pack to wear as river shoes. They add weight to my load, but I've learned it's worth carrying those additional ounces. Besides, sneakers double as good "waders" for fishing and triple as quick-drying camp slippers.

Waterproofing Your Pack

If you are of the poncho persuasion, a long version of this item worn over you and your pack will keep both fairly dry on the trail. But a backpack exposed directly to rain needs, at the least, further waterproofing. You'd be best off to buy or improvise a waterproof cover. Recreational Equipment, Inc., carries rain covers that come in small, medium, and large sizes for external frame packs and medium or large for internal frame packs. And Kelty has something that really takes the cake: the Rubber Duckie. It's a combination poncho, packcover, and personal tent. Yes, you heard it here first, folks, but you have to see it (perhaps even try to figure out how to use it, maybe in a stiff wind) to believe it.

Backpackers who prefer economy and improvisation can get by

with a heavy-duty plastic garbage bag over the pack. Cut a rectangular panel out of the back of the plastic so the pack's shoulder straps stick out, and carry an extra bag in case the first one rips. It most likely will.

Any Wet Trail

Whether you're cycling, canoeing, or hiking, some wet-travel concerns are common to all.

Maps

Trails and contour lines seem to disappear with surprising ease from a map that gets wet. A plastic map holder with a zipper will take a folded topographic map that can be read without having to remove it from the case. Almost as effective is any large, clear plastic bag with plenty of room at the top to fold over several times. Keep the top folded down by putting an elastic band around the bag. A bag with a zip-lock top is even better.

Camera

Photographs can capture the essence of nature's wet-weather offerings: mist hanging in the sugar palms, water strung on a stalk of wild grass, a rainbow, or the looming roll of thunderheads. But a water-logged camera doesn't capture these or any other scenes very well.

I've found that if I don't keep my camera where I can get at it readily—either slung on the outside of my pack or around my neck—I never get around to taking the photographs I know I should. That means some waterproofing is necessary.

Unfortunately, the case for my camera is bulky enough to be bothersome. So instead, I use a sturdy plastic bag with holes cut in the corners through which I run the camera straps. The bag covers the camera until a good photo opportunity appears. Then I slide the plastic bag up the strap, and the camera is ready for use. It's helpful to reinforce the strap holes in the bag with duct tape or adhesive tape. This precaution will greatly reduce the chance of tearing the plastic, and it will provide a snug fit around the straps.

Condensation can also be a problem in rainy weather. It's caused when the camera is first warmed next to your body or beneath your clothing and is then suddenly exposed to cooler air. The lens and viewfinder become so fogged up that the moose you're trying to photograph looks like smoke in a thick mist. The solution is to keep the camera at the same temperature as the outside air. This means keeping it away from your body heat, either hung outside your clothes or, if even that's too warm, slung from your pack.

As for film, Kodak 35mm rolls come in plastic containers with snap-on tops. These should be all the protection the film will need, even if you plan on taking it for a swim. Other types of film should be sealed in double plastic bags.

Assorted Plastic Bags

You'll notice that I mention plastic bags a lot. Well, when it's wet, they have lots of uses, not the least of which is in bagging food, clothes, and sleeping gear before putting them into your pack, pannier, or box. This bagging will provide double protection and will keep your clothes dry when you rummage through your open pack looking for that candy bar that has fallen to the bottom.

Assorted Biting Bugs

Wet environs have a habit of breeding biting bugs, particularly mosquitoes. And, as luck would have it, mosquitoes are especially fond of poking their proboscises into hot, wet, huffing hikers, bikers, and canoeists. In fact, studies have shown that the carbon dioxide from your breath alerts a mosquito to your presence. Warmth and moisture from your skin (particularly warm and moist when you're active) further help mosquitoes zero in on you. Black flies and no-see-ums have even worse reputations than mosquitoes. They, also, hang around in squadrons where the ground is wet and marshy.

Dealing with these creatures is largely a matter of a fast hand and the use of diethyl-meta-toluamide, the major active ingredient in the most effective insects repellents like Off and Cutter. Some people find that vitamin B1 taken orally helps discourage mosquitoes. And phenolated calamine lotion will reduce itching when applied to bites.

Sometimes nothing seems to help. I have the vivid memory of a wooden camping platform raised a foot above the Okefenokee Swamp. When the sun went down on the wilderness canoe trail, the mosquitoes came out, and they came out, and they came out. To this day I have an image of the four of us pacing the platform while spooning dinner and mosquitoes into our mouths. The tent was our only refuge, but only after locating and dispatching the dozens of eager eaters that entered when we did.

In the morning sunlight, not a mosquito was to be seen.

A campsite is more than a place to pitch a tent. It's part of the rhythm of the landscape.

Wet-Weather Campsite

A campsite is more than a place to pitch a tent. It's part of the rhythm of the landscape. Tamper with that rhythm and the scene is out of step with the natural world, even after you have disappeared and forgotten the spot. Consequently, a major concern in any kind of weather is to have minimum impact on the land and leave it looking as untouched as possible.

Selecting a good campsite is largely a matter of finding a place that will do the most for you without your doing much to it. It should be clear that gullies, hollows, dry washes, and other natural drainages are not very agreeable locations (see page 76) when they start to collect water. Instead, look for high ground that offers some natural protection from the prevailing winds. The lee side of a ridge, boulder, or unexposed ledge can often break the wind enough to keep rain from blowing in the windows and door of your tent or under the sides of your tarp. A forested area will also offer more protection than an open field, although the rain often drips from the trees for hours after a storm has passed. Hilltops and knolls can be windy, while valley side hills will provide more protection.

Occasionally you can find complete natural shelter under a large boulder, ledge, or overhang. In the canyon country of Utah, I once

Take advantage of natural shelters whenever possible.

camped in the dry confines of a deep overhang while rain pelted the sandstone and thunder tumbled off the surrounding walls. I could hardly have been more comfortable had I been curled up in my bed at home.

Once you've found protection from the rain, consider the matter of convenience. Is a source of cooking water close enough to save you from a drenching walk in the rain? Do trees offer a handy arrangement for pitching a tarp? Can you find plenty of downed, dead, and dry firewood?

The more of these natural features you can combine in one location, the more comfortable you'll be living there. Don't discount matters of aesthetics either. Pleasant scenery, whether a solitary tree in fall color or the reach of a cloud-shrouded ridge, can elevate the spirit even if you are peeking out from a tent or a tarp.

There are, of course, areas where officially designated campsites have been established or where obvious unofficial sites have developed. These spots aren't always the most attractive places to camp. However, it's usually easier on the landscape to use an existing site rather than establish one that isn't needed. There are exceptions. "Closed to Camping' signs, often placed in areas that have been used too heavily, should be respected. Also avoid camping within 100 feet of lakes and streams and in alpine meadows. Vegetation in these areas is particularly susceptible to damage and will deteriorate quickly with repeated use.

A Tent for the Rain

Sleeping beneath the stars is a fine way to fully appreciate the natural world. Sleeping under clouds when they leak is simply a way of testing the moisture-absorbing capacity of yourself and your sleeping bag. Any New Englander will tell you that. It's true that a tent will probably be the single heaviest item in your pack. Yet when there's the possibility of rain, wind, and biting bugs, a properly pitched tent may be the only thing between you and raving lunacy. From inside, snug and dry, you can watch the rest of the world swirl in the deluge.

Single-Walled vs. Double-Walled Tents

At one time, all tents were made with a single layer of fabric. But the problem with fully waterproof single-walled tents has traditionally been that of condensation. Warm air inside these tents comes into contact with the cool walls, where moisture collects and can't escape.

The moisture drips down upon, or is rubbed off on, your clothes and sleeping bag, making you damp and miserable.

The apparent answer is to use a material that will let condensation out but prevent rain coming in. For years, canvas was that material. At first moisture, the threads expand, closing out water droplets but letting water vapor escape. If, however, you touch the inside of a canvas tent, you will cause it to leak at that point. Canvas is too heavy for backpackers and bicyclists, and not the best choice for canoeists.

Breathable waterproof material in the late '70s looked promising for single-walled tents. But its use in tents has had mixed reviews from harsh weather campers in the 1980s. The big complaint is that it doesn't solve the condensation problem. The tent walls are too far away from the occupants for the "vapor pressure" from their perspiration to push moisture through the fabric. Without this extra push from body heat, water vapor condenses inside the tent. Other campers, however, claim they don't experience this problem.

Despite the availability of breathable waterproof material in tents, most still use the double-walled system. Here the upper walls and roof of the tent itself are made of uncoated nylon, but the floor and the bottom 6 to 12 inches of the walls areof coated, waterproof nylon. Water vapor inside the tent can evaporate through the uncoated weave of the roof. But a second layer—a waterproof roof, or rainfly— is needed to keep the rain from coming in. This rainfly is suspended several inches above the roof of the tent to allow for the escape of water vapor into the intervening air space. Since the inner layer of a double-walled tent tends to be warmer than the outer layer, most condensation collects on the cooler outer layer, where it runs off to the ground. Some condensation, however, may form between your foam sleeping pad and the tent's waterproof floor.

Livability

Studies have demonstrated and experience has proven that cramped, noisy, and harsh-colored tents will increase your fatigue and irritability. This is never more true than when you are confined to quarters for long periods of time by totally disagreeable downpours. So you'll do well to look for a tent that has features to enhance its wet-weather livability.

• *Size*—A tent that you can't sit up in will not be suitable for much more than sleeping. And while a two-man tent may be eminently satisfactory for two snoring people, those same people awake would

A tent in the rain can be either a comfortable refuge from the elements or a cramped, noisy hovel. Select a model with an eye to wet-weather livability.

be much more comfortable in a space that could hold three. Two-man tents to which vestibules can be attached may alleviate cramping because gear can be stored out of the way. Otherwise, you're better off using a tent that can accommodate at least one more person than the number who will be calling it home.

• *Design*—Living space in a tent is also influenced by design. Tunnel and dome tents can offer as much as 50% more living room than A-frame tents having the same floor dimensions. Your view and ventilation can also be affected by design. Look for a tent in which storm doors and windows can be left partly open, for air and scenery, without letting rain enter. This goal is accomplished by having plenty of roof overhang. Yet a tent with an all-encompassing rain fly may keep you dry without letting you see anything of the outside world. Unfortunately, many dome tents have this problem.

A tent that flaps noisily in the wind can seem like Chinese water torture. So it's helpful to have design features that minimize this tendency. An A-frame design is probably the best on this score, but any tent that can be pitched so that all panels are tight, including the rainfly, will remain reasonably quiet.

Another design aspect to look for is the ease with which a tent can be erected. Flyless tents and those that have rainflys permanently attached to the inner tent are handy in this respect. A tent with a minimum number of pegs, poles, and guy lines will also reduce the time you must spend out in the rain setting it up. Some of the new Gore-Tex dome tents even have internal pole systems that allow you to get in out of the rain while you're still putting things together.

• *Color*—The color of a tent has a big influence on your mood. Since you're the only one who knows what colors have positive or negative effects on you, you'll have to do the choosing. A few general points, however, are worth keeping in mind. Dark colors under cloudy skies tend to be gloomy when viewed from inside a tent. Bright colors, on the other hand, give a bizarre cast to your companion's complexion and really blast your eyeballs when the sun comes out. Natural or subdued colors are your best bet for letting in plenty of light and subtly reinforcing a positive outlook on a damp day. Besides it's been my experience that tan, white, and light green are not very attractive to flesh-chewing bugs. Blue seems to attract them in droves.

Tarp

Where bugs are few and rain is light or infrequent, a tarp will offer adequate protection while cutting down on the weight you must carry.

The use of a tarp as a shelter can cut down considerably on your weight.

I've camped many a spring and fall night in the great Basin Desert where a low-slung tarp kept off rain, sleet, and some snow. Even if I don't plan on sleeping under a tarp, the use of one to make a dry kitchen has become indispensable for my wet-weather bag of procedures.

The most basic variety of tarp is made of clear .004-inch plastic sheet. It lets plenty of light in and allows you to get a somewhat distorted view of your surroundings. Sizes from 7' x 9' to 12' x 12' are the most efficient. Pebbles tied into the plastic with cords can keep guy lines from slipping off, or you can buy gadgets like Vis-Clamps (rubber balls and wire loops that lock into the plastic) to serve the same purpose.

A more permanent tarp would be one of coated nylon with grommets at the corners and along the edges. Some models have pullout tabs at various locations over the surface of the tarp. Moss Tents has a wonderfully designed 12-foot dining fly called the Parawing. It weighs less than two pounds, is easy to pitch, and is stable in a wind, but it checks in at around $100. At the other extreme, two ponchos can be snapped together to form a crude pup tent, but this is only an emergency measure.

Pitching Tents and Tarps Against the Rain

Pitching Tents

Tents generally are designed to go up only one way. But what you use to put one up and how you position the tent in relation to the wind may make the difference between comfort and calamity.

First, not all tent pegs were created equal. The pegs that look like sawed-off barbeque skewers may be compact and light, but they won't hold in most kinds of wet ground. Just when you get to sleep, one of these pegs is going to pull out and your house is going to sag. Before long, you'll feel as if you're a part of a cat fight in a wet bag.

To avoid such a situation, use either plastic pegs with a T-shaped cross section or aluminum pegs with a U-shaped cross section. The U-shaped variety are more compact because they nest together. Rocks, trees, and bushes can also be used where they're willing to cooperate and the regulations allow it.

Position your tent with an eye to the wind. Usually your entrance should be pitched facing away from the wind. This orientation offers some protection from blowing rain while you're getting in and out. With an A-frame or tunnel design, it also presents a minimum surface area to the wind and allows air to scoop under the tent's rainfly, ballooning it out instead of plastering it up against the inner wall, where it could cause condensation to leak through. At all times, pitch a rainfly as taut as possible to help prevent it from touching the inner tent layer. Some of the new, exotic-shaped tents may be exceptions to pitching the entrance away from the wind since this positioning may mean putting the tent's largest surface area into the wind. Under really windy conditions, all tents should be equipped with shock cords on the guy lines. Otherwise, undue stress is put on tent stitching and materials.

Pitching Tarps

The way you pitch a tarp against the rain depends on the type of rain. Drizzle, sprinkles, or light rain can be handled with a simple A-frame arrangement. A steady rain and wind will call for pitching one end of the tarp low against the wind with the other end high enough to provide some head room. A very tight, but somewhat claustrophobic arrangement can be made with one edge of a tarp attached to the side of an overturned canoe and the opposite edge anchored to the ground. Any number of the other configurations can be rigged to fit specific situations.

You can convert your canoe and your paddles into a shelter with the use of a tarp.

A tarp can be an effective shelter against the rain. Pitch one end low against the wind and the other end high for headroom.

• *Ditching a Tarp*—digging a little moat around a tarp to prevent ground water from seeping under is an outdated practice because of the mess it can make of the ground cover. If you get caught in a heavy rain, either be smugly Spartan and endure the undertarp trickles, or dig a small ditch with a pricked conscience and replace the soil before you leave the site.

Sleeping Gear

It has been said that you can face almost anything if you've had a good night's sleep. Heard less frequently, but just as true, is that piece of backwoods wisdom that says "sleep does not come to the soggy." Now, a snug shelter goes a long way toward keeping you dry, but a wet-weather sleeping bag and pad are needed to complete the protection.

Sleeping Bags

Paul Petzoldt, founder and director of the National Outdoor Leadership School, said it years ago—the only way to go into rain or snow is polyester. Lots of folks laughed at the idea. Others said they agreed, that they, too, would carry a polyester bag if planning to camp in the rain or be atop the Grand Teton on New Year's Day, but that most people were not into wet-weather camping or winter mountaineering. Well, when it comes to rain, anyone thinking of doing much camping in the Northeast or Northwest at any time had better consider the possibility of "getting into" wet-weather camping. The southern Appalachians have been known to be a bit damp on occasion, too, as have Minnesota and any number of other hiking, biking, and canoeing spots. In these places, you're wise to have a polyester sleeping bag.

Polyester has the distinct advantages of: absorbing almost no moisture, retaining a high percentage of loft (insulating thickness) when damp, and drying quickly. Another advantage is polyester's price. A glance at catalogs indicates that a polyester bag cost about half as much as a down bag.

There are disadvantages to polyester, to be sure. It requires 15 to 20 percent more fill by weight to get the same loft as top-grade down. In addition, polyester fibers don't compress as well as down, although they are as resilient. So a polyester bag is both bulkier and heavier than a down bag in a similar warmth range. Yet a polyester bag can still meet the requirements of most backpackers and cyclists, and canoeists don't have to be concerned about its weight or bulk.

These claims in the name of polyester assume that a quality fill is being used and that the bag is designed for self-propelled campers.

Of the two grades of polyester—branded and unbranded—branded is the kind that competes favorably with top-grade down, and is quality controlled to meet the standards of a polyester sleeping-bag filler. Currently, the most widely used, brand-name fillers are Polar Guard, Quallofil, and Hollofil II.

The design of the bag is important. For years, polyester was used to make those heavy, voluminous bags that were suitable only for car camping. But today you'll find lighter, more streamlined models, which are intended for backpacking and cycling.

"What about down?" someone is undoubtedly asking. It's true that some people would gladly shell out the extra money in order to get the benefits of a down bag's high-quality performance. Down is more compressible than any other sleeping-bag filler. It can be compressed into one-seventh of its fluffed-up size, yet it's resilient enough to spring back into shape repeatedly. And it has a nicer feel than synthetic fillers.

Unfortunately, down has one real drawback—it absorbs moisture easily, whether from sweat, condensation, or rain. And once the down gets wet, it loses much of its insulative value. Furthermore, down takes days to dry out completely. It's one thing to throw a bag into a commercial dryer; it's something else to try drying a down bag in a rain-choked camp. The use of a breathable waterproof sleeping-bag shell can prevent moisture's entry from the outside, but humidity, condensation, and sweat still remain a problem, unless you use a vapor barrier (see page 132), and that makes you too hot. So, wet weather still deserves polyester in my book.

Sleeping Pads

Like down bags, sleeping pads (usually polyurethane) can become giant sponges. Thick open-cell foam pads—the ones almost everyone buys—are the worst offenders. Most of these pads are covered with waterproof material on the bottom and breathable material on the top. This arrangement helps somewhat, but moisture still seems to get trapped in the pad during rainy weather. Many campers are willing to put up with this problem—particularly if they have a polyester sleeping bag—in order to get the two inches of softness that only an open cell foam pad can offer.

By contrast, closed-cell pads of polyvinyl chloride, polyethylene, and ethylene-vinyl-acetate are, for all intents, impervious to water and don't need a cover. Yet for many campers, a firm half-inch mattress of such material is not considered very comfortable.

It's important to remember, however, that polyester sleeping bags—because they don't compress as much as down bags—will offer quite a bit of cushioning by themselves. In fact, some manufacturers of polyester bags claim their products are comfortable in most seasons without the extra cushioning and insulation of a sleeping pad.

Another possibility, in temperatures above about 40°F., is an air mattress. If you tried previous versions you're likely to remember a deflating letdown in the middle of the night. Things have changed. Except for the all-vinyl cheapies, good vinyl/nylon or vinyl/rayon laminated mattresses are available and are quite tough. But carry an appropriate repair kit just in case.

Out of the Rain, In a Tent

Camping in rainy weather, by chance or plan, doesn't doom you to spend all your time in a tent. But there are times when you'll find that's the most desirable place to be. And there are some things you can do to make your stay inside enjoyable.

Probably your first concern should be to leave the moisture outside where it belongs. A tent alcove or tarp pitched at the tent entrance as a kind of front porch comes in handy here. Wet boots and rain clothes can be removed while you are under cover but still not within the tent proper. Then moisture from your raingear doesn't drip all over sleeping bags or the tent floor, and yet the rain clothes are readily available when you exit.

Once in the tent, you can't avoid some dampness in the air. Every time you exhale, moisture is added to the environment. And in humid parts of the country, dampness is a standard element in that tent environment. You can cut down on the problem by mopping up any obvious moisture on floor and walls. Carry a sponge in a plastic bag for the purpose, and keep the sponge sealed in the bag when it's not in use. Also keep any wet clothes wrapped in plastic when they're in the tent.

Even though sleeping bags are supposed to be fluffed up in order to attain their maximum loft, it's smart to keep them in their waterproof stuff sacks until ready for use. Otherwise, they'll absorb moisture from the air, particularly if they are filled with down.

Just because you're in a tent doesn't mean you have to go to sleep. I've spent many a contented hour reading beneath a tent roof, and some long-delayed letters have turned into lengthy missives there. More than once a clamorous philosophical debate or an amorous embrace has been inspired by the pat-tapping of rain on a tent roof. Eventually, however, even the most preoccupying activities get interrupted by a stomach's growl.

Wet-Weather Kitchen

Any camper in the rain should have a protected kitchen, and a tent is not the place to have it (see page 164). The key ingredient for the kitchen is a large, coated-nylon tarp; 12′ × 12′ is a roomy size. This can be set up anywhere the landscape provides suitable tie-downs. Of course, your selection of a campsite was done with this in mind. Canoeists have an advantage over hikers and bikers because paddles come in handy for supporting one or more corners of the tarp. Fallen, dead poles can also be used. But chopping down live saplings for the purpose of pitching a tarp is just a stupid and unnecessary waste of scenery.

A tarp pitched for a kitchen roof will go a long way toward making your wet-weather camp comfortable.

A variety of roofs can be made with the tarp. Wind permitting, try to keep your ceiling high enough to stand under. You'll find the kitchen will also become the diningroom, livingroom, standingroom, and bicycle repair shop. Cord can be used as a center ridgepole, with the tarp sloping down on each side. The cord also acts as an under-cover clothesline.

Another choice is to slope the tarp on one plane like a lean-to roof. Or you can use a deadwood pole with some padding on the top to make a center post from which the tarp's sides slope down all around.

A really taut kitchen roof will keep rain from puddling on it. On the other hand, it's pretty convenient to have a pure water supply right on your roof where only the push of a hand will pour water into a well-placed pot.

However you decide to pitch your tarp, you'll find that it offers one of the most companionable spaces in your camp. The cook can spread out and still leave room for others to come in out of the rain. Rocks and logs provide seats that, when turned over so the dry side is up, won't dampen your pants. If you prefer, you can carry a small square of closed-cell foam or use your sleeping pad to provide a dry and insulated seat. Under the tarp, gear can be dried, stories told, and coffee sipped while you view the scenery without being out in what's coming down.

Stove vs. Fire

A lightweight cook stove will readily produce hot meals or just coffee without your having to start a fire. But a fire will warm your body and spirit and dry your clothes the way no stove ever can.

One problem with a fire is getting ample dry firewood from a sod-den forest. Another problem is ethics. Can you build and maintain a fire without appreciably scarring the surroundings? In a dense forest with vigorous growth, or on a beach where driftwood constantly washes ashore, the fuel you use won't be missed. But at timberline or in a sparse piñon forest or in any heavily used area, gathering fire-wood can lead to an unnatural mess. Hacked-up stumps and broken stubs where dead branches once hung can hardly add to the scenic subtleties of a campsite. Even where wood is plentiful, smoke-black-ened rocks and fire rings only remind you of those who've come be-fore, when you'd like to pretend you were the first one around. So whether or not you build a fire must be a choice of conscience.

I believe a stove should be packed along for cooking. What type of stove you take in rainy weather matters little, except for alcohol stoves, which have too low a heat output to be useful under such conditions. Canoeists may be able to carry a two-burner or even three-burner camp stove for preparing multi-course meals. Otherwise, you are limited to taking one of the many single-burner models.

No matter what kind of stove you take, its efficiency will be greatly diminished by wind. Some stoves come with built-in wind screens; others will require improvisation. Backpacks, the lee of a large rock, or aluminum foil crimped around a semicircle of sticks stuck in the ground can all serve as windbreaks. Do not, however, surround a stove too closely. Abnormal heat build-up can cause an explosion.

Where appropriate, a fire may also be desirable. You don't need a roaring bonfire. A small compact fire with lots of hot coals will throw off plenty of heat and burn much less wood. The ideal placement of a fire is at the downwind edge of your kitchen tarp. Here it will be protected from the rain and will still let some heat rise up under the roof. Yet smoke will not collect there. As for the fireplace itself, unless it can be built on sand or bare ground, it's best to build it *in* the ground.

Carefully remove a 12″ × 16″ block of sod and place it aside. Then

For the sake of the surroundings, build your fire in the ground instead of on top of it—if you must have a fire. Replace the soil and sod when you break camp.

dig down to mineral soil, placing what you remove over the ground cover around the hole. This precaution will help protect the vegetation from scorching. Dampness from the weather should be enough to prevent fire danger from any other vegetation in the vicinity. When you are ready to leave camp, drown the fire, fill in the hole, and carefully replace the sod. After you've scattered any remaining firewood that's been gathered, and after you've packed up everything that you brought in with you including all scraps of garbage, the place should look just about as natural as when you found it.

Fire Starters

You may be able to gather plenty of dead wood. But starting a fire, particularly if the wood is damp, is the tricky matter. First, you'll need a reliable source of flame. Big kitchen matches are the old standby. A bunch of these can be carried in a waterproof match case, but you probably won't be able to get enough into it to last an entire trip. However, an easy way to make these matches waterproof—a trick I learned as a kid preparing for a canoe trip on Ontario's French River—is to dip each match in melted paraffin. By immersing the entire match, first one end and then the other, you'll seal out all moisture. These matches can be stored in a plastic bag for further protection.

Waterproof and windproof matches are available commercially, but these must be struck on the waterproof striker attached to the box they come in.

Other fire and stove starters are available. Cigarette lighters are usually okay when kept filled with fuel and provided with an extra flint. But I'll never forget one fateful whitewater trip down the Middle Fork of Montana's Flathead River when I found myself in the drink with my two companions. When we reached shore, soaked and bedraggled, we couldn't get a lighter to work. But a "Permanent Match" did. The device consists of a reservoir of lighter fluid into which the permanent match is screwed. To ignite the wick on this match, you unscrew it and strike it against the flint striking pad. Another such device is the "Metal Match." It is a rod composed of oxides that can be shaved off for tinder and ignited with a spark made by striking the match with your knife or the special striker provided.

Other fire-making accessories designed to help urge wet wood into warmth include Fire Ribbon, a flammable paste that burns for several minutes; and candle stubs with lots of stearic acid in them to insure long burning time. Leave a candle burning under twigs and kindling long enough and they are bound to make a fire that will warm your toes, dry your clothes, and fill everything with the basic essence of wood smoke.

It was just that smoky smell that caught the nose of the gal who gave my wife and me a ride back to our car after a damp and blustery canoe trip on Arrow Lake, British Columbia.

"You've been camping, haven't you? I can smell it," she announced after we'd been in the car only a few minutes. "It must have been an awful wet trip with this weather we've been having. Sure glad *I* wasn't out in that stuff."

In fact, "that stuff" *had* been wet. But we'd gone prepared with proper clothes and equipment, and we'd done more than stand around a fire soaking up smoke.

One highlight of the trip was the catching of four large rainbow trout on four casts in a pelting rain. I'm convinced the rain had something to do with this fantastic luck. But it didn't pour for the entire trip. We had drizzle for exploring an abandoned homestead with moss on its roof and the deep green of lush vegetation pushing at its door. Through intermittent showers we watched otters gamboling near the shore and black bear lumbering through the bush. And a steady, light rain accompanied many of our paddle strokes. It was a memorable trip, and we were glad to have taken it, to some degree *because* of the weather.

4

Wet-Weather Hazards

Despite other opinions people have about wet weather, it's not often considered dangerous. Yet each year a number of people die from hypothermia, lightning, and flash floods. Many of these fatalities could have been prevented if the victims had known what to look for and how to respond. Any well-prepared outdoors person should have the knowledge to cope wisely with these wet-weather phenomena.

Hypothermia

I'd seen the symptoms many times before, but this was the first time they were showing on me. We were 20 miles from the nearest road, careening down the Middle Fork of Montana's Flathead River. I was wet and tired and wracked with involuntary and uncontrollable shivers. Those shivers were the start of an often irreversible loss of inner body heat—a phenomenon called hypothermia.

There was only one thing to do: get off the river, change into dry clothes, build a fire, and have some hot food and liquid.

That incident happened in July when the air temperature was close to 50°F., but I could have died from the cold.

There is no doubt that the increased interest in hiking, biking, and canoeing has caused a sharp rise in deaths from hypothermia. So organizations such as the U.S. Forest Service, the National Park Service, the U.S. Skiing Association, and even some insurance companies have been attempting, through films and booklets, to acquaint the outdoor public with the real danger of this hazard. Probably the best known booklet on the subject, written by Theodore G. Lathrop, M.D., is titled *Hypothermia: Killer of the Unprepared.*

Hypothermia is caused when your body loses heat faster than it can produce heat. When this situation first occurs, blood vessels in your skin constrict in an attempt to conserve vital internal heat. Hands and feet are the first areas affected.

If your body continues to lose heat, involuntary shivers begin. This is your body's way of attempting to produce more heat, and it is usually the first real warning sign of hypothermia. Continued unchecked, further heat loss (and the resulting decrease in body temperature) produces speech difficulty, forgetfulness, loss of manual dexterity, collapse, and finally death. All this can happen in a frighteningly short time.

That's what hypothermia does, and here's a typical example of how it can come about. A sixteen-year-old goes out for an afternoon hike clad in bluejeans and a cotton T-shirt. He's tired from staying up the night before, and he has skipped lunch. But it's spring. The day feels warm, and it's good to get away from the homework awhile. As he climbs a familiar ridge, clouds begin to pile up, and within an hour a light rain is falling. His clothes get damp, but exercise keeps him warm until the sun slides behind the ridge. Then he gets chilled. The downhill hike going back only makes things worse. By the time he gets home, he's shivering and has difficulty speaking.

Without knowing it, the teenager is in the first stages of hypothermia. But he's fortunate. He can go into a warm house where a hot bath and food and drink reverse the downward spiral of heat loss. If he had gone a little further from home, however, he might not have been so lucky.

A closer look at this real incident will help clarify the causes of hypothermia and what can be done to prevent it.

Cold

Your body's sense of cold depends on several factors. The thermometer may read 48 degrees F., and the possibility of hypothermia may seem as remote as snowballs in hell. But many a recorded case of "exposure" has occurred in temperatures well above freezing. How cold your body gets depends not only on air temperature but also on all of the following factors.

Physical Condition

Food consumption and exercise are your body's way of producing heat and energy. The teenager in the case just cited hadn't eaten since breakfast and consequently had little fuel for his body's furnace. He was engaged in strenuous exercise, which is a heat producer but also a fuel consumer. In addition he was tired, a further strain on his body's ability to function efficiently.

Had he been well rested and properly nourished, he might not have experienced the first stages of hypothermia. For this reason it is important to be well rested and well fed when hiking in wet and cool weather. Forget about the diet you are supposed to be on (unless it's prescribed by a physician) and take along quick-energy snacks—nuts, jerky, candy—for munching on the trail.

Dampness

Moisture on your skin and in your clothes can conduct heat away from your body many times faster than you'd lose it under normal conditions. Besides, some materials lose almost all of their insulative value when wet. Polypropylene and polyester clothes do not. Wear them. Forget blue jeans; pure cotton soaks up water like a sponge.

Your main concern, however, is to stay as dry as possible. Rain (or snow) gear in the form of water-resistant parka and pants will go a long way in keeping the moisture out. Waterproof clothing is good when you aren't active, but will cause inner condensation when you exercise. Waterproof/breathable clothing is best.

Sweat is another moisture causer, and it's difficult to avoid when you're active. The only effective way to keep perspiration to a minimum is to open up or take off clothes when you are active. For the best thermostatic control, wear layers of shirt, sweater, and light parka. In this way you can take off different garments in order to control body heat. With one heavy parka over a shirt, you will probably end up too hot or too cold.

Wind

Heat loss from wind convection is probably the greatest and most deceptive factor in loss of body heat. It's especially dangerous for the cyclist. When the air is still and its temperature is 30°F., you'll feel cool. In air of the same temperature that's blowing 25 m.p.h., you'll feel bitterly cold. Wind blows away the thin layer of air that has been

warmed by your body and would normally act as an insulator between your skin and the outside air. If you and your clothing are wet,
the cooling effect of the wind is even stronger.

WIND-CHILL TABLE								
Wind *(mph)*	*Actual Temperature in* °F							
	40	30	20	10	0	−10	−20	−30
	Equivalent Chill Temperature							
Calm	40	30	20	10	0	−10	−20	−30
5	35	25	15	5	−5	−15	−25	−35
10	30	15	5	−10	−20	−35	−45	−60
15	25	10	−5	−20	−30	−45	−60	−70
20	20	5	−10	−25	−35	−50	−65	−80
25	15	0	−15	−30	−45	−60	−75	−90
30	10	0	−20	−30	−50	−65	−80	−95
35	10	−5	−20	−35	−50	−65	−80	−100
40	10	−5	−20	−35	−55	−70	−85	−100

To counter the effects of convection, close-woven parka and pants
are a must; these can come in the form of rain gear. Make sure they
can be closed snugly around ankles, wrists, and waist. Also use a
parka with a hood, and wear a wool hat beneath it. Body heat escapes
fast from your unprotected head and neck.

Your chances of avoiding hypothermia are good if you're aware of
the effects of cold, physical conditioning, dampness, and wind and if
you protect yourself with proper food, rest, and clothing. But, as I've
discovered, no one is immune to hypothermia. So you'd better know
what to do about it if it strikes.

• First, know the symptoms of hypothermia: involuntary shivering,
difficulty in speech, forgetfulness, loss of manual dexterity, stumbling,
and collapse. The shivering will probably come first. Don't ignore it.

• Anyone displaying any of these signs should immediately be shel-
tered from wind, rain, or snow. A lightweight tarp or tube tent can
easily be carried; even in a day pack, and could be a life saver.

• Take off the victim's wet clothing, and get him into dry clothes if
he is conscious and able to cooperate. Then get him into a warm
sleeping bag, if it's available, or sandwich him between companions in
order to supply external warmth. Hot liquid and food will provide
additional warmth, so think about carrying emergency provisions and

Uncontrollable shivering may be the first sign of hypothermia. Don't ignore it. Get the victim warm by any means available.

a light cook stove or a can of Sterno whenever you go out, even for a day trip.

• If the person is unconscious, strip off his clothes and get him into a sleeping bag or wrap him in dry parkas or clothing with another person or several people who have also stripped. The important thing is to apply external heat since the victim can't generate his own heat. A warming fire should also be started. As soon as the victim is conscious, get him to drink hot liquids.

These are the emergency procedures you should take against hypothermia. If you follow proper precautions and use common sense, hypothermia shouldn't happen.

Lightning

Cyclists who travel through an Arizona summer must keep on the lookout for flash floods during the inevitable afternoon thunderstorm. In Vermont, a similar summer storm dampens your sleeping bag even as it offers some respite from the heat. And somewhere in the Sierra Nevada, a hiker cringes at a crack of thunder as it ricochets off canyon walls. Yet a thunderstorm is more than a deafening noise.

The spark in the storm should be your greatest concern, particularly when you consider that as many as 500 lightning fatalities and 1,300 lightning injuries occur annually. Anyone who will be out in the sound and the fury of an electrical storm ought to know something about lightning and how to minimize its dangers.

The basic mechanism for lightning is created in the formation of cumulonimbus clouds that become charged with electricity in a way scientists still do not understand. The top part of a thunderhead becomes positively charged and the bottom becomes negatively charged. In addition, the negative charge in the base of the clouds induces a positive charge in the ground below it. This positive charge flows up high objects on land and water trying to make contact with the negative charges in the thunderhead.

The electrical potential of a thunderhead grows until the attracting power of the two areas of opposite electrical charges causes one charge to rush to the other. Lightning, the huge electrical spark that results, may contain 15 million volts as it jumps from cloud to cloud, cloud to earth, or from earth to cloud.

As powerful as these lightening bolts can be, they are resisted by the air itself; usually a good insulator. But when a high enough electrical pressure is built up in the clouds, even the air becomes electrically charged—a process called ionization. The ionizing process destroys the insulating properties of air and produces an unstable form of oxygen called ozone. The pungent smell of ozone is a certain indicator that you are in an area where lightning may be imminent. In addition, as air ionizes around a conductor of electricity, such as a rock, metal, or even a person, it may cause a bluish halo called St. Elmo's Fire. If your head happens to be the conductor, your hair will stand on end and crackle. It is a frightening and unmistakable sign that you'd better seek safer ground immediately.

As potent as the smell of ozone and the sight of St. Elmo's Fire are as indicators of immediate danger from lightning, plan to take some defensive action *before* you end up in the middle of a thunderstorm.

To start with, count the seconds between a lightning flash and the ensuing crash of thunder. You'll gain a sense of the distance between you and the fireworks. Sight travels faster than sound, and every 5 seconds between the flash and the bang indicates one mile. If you can see that the storm clouds will miss you, there's little to worry about. But when the storm is obviously moving your way, you should do something. The typical thunderstorm travels a mile every two or three minutes, so you shouldn't try to outrun one. Yet knowing something about lightning's habits will enable you to seek out the least dangerous location nearby.

Since lightning takes the line of least resistance, it will always strike a conductor that is prominent and close, although a spark between a cloud and the earth may be as long as 8 miles. The conductor may be the ground, a rock, or a tree. Metal and the human body are even better conductors. And any of these objects are more subject to a lightning strike if they are wet.

A direct hit is not the only danger. Lightning is further hazardous because it spreads out in all directions on the ground, dissipating its power as it goes. As it travels, it continues to follow the line of least resistance. Therefore, it usually moves over the surface of rocks, especially if they are wet. It will flow along damp crevices, streams, and moisture-holding vegetation. When lightning comes to narrow gaps in rocks or small depressions in the ground, it often arcs across them instead of going around a longer route.

All these characteristics suggest places you should avoid when lightning is near. Although it's often impossible in the middle of a storm, avoid wet areas if you can, particularly crevices and narrow depressions. Both the top and the base of a cliff are dangerous; the top because it's exposed, the bottom because it's subject to an electrical ground charge. Any exposed shoulders or faces in the terrain are also unsafe. Shallow caves or recesses offer tempting cover but may be the location of a ground arc. It should be clear that a mountain top and hill top as well as a lone or tall tree is a prime target for lightning strikes and should be avoided. Likewise, avoid large, flat open areas where you are the most prominent object. Canoeists, in other words, had better *get off the water.*

Although it may sound as if 90 percent of the landscape is unsafe during an electrical storm, there are really many places to seek refuge. In a forest, your best bet is to find a clump of trees shorter than the surrounding trees and remain there until the storm passes. Any low point in the terrain that covers a large area, such as a valley, is a good spot to be. If you happen to be stuck on a ridge, try to get to the middle of it rather than to either end. When you're near a cliff, stay at least 50 feet from its base but not so far away as to become the most prominent object around.

Once you've reached the spot where you plan to wait out the storm, you should do several things to further protect yourself. It's important to keep as much of your body off the ground as possible while still maintaining a low position. Hunker down on your feet, keeping them close together and keeping your hands off the ground. Sitting exposes more of your body to possible ground charges, and lying is even worse. If possible, get some dry insulation between you and the ground. A foam pad, a sleeping bag, or a coil of climbing rope will work. However, stay out of contact with metal objects such as pack frame, camera, or knife. Finally, don't huddle together in a group. Stay 40 to 50 feet apart. This way, if one person is injured by lightning, it's probable that others will be unharmed and able to apply first aid.

What *do* you do if someone is struck by lightning? The first concern is the patient's heartbeat and breathing which may have stopped. Although the heart may begin again on its own, breathing often will not. In any case, check immediately for those vital life signs. If necessary, apply external heart message or mouth-to-mouth resuscitation. Once heartbeat and breathing are restored, treat for shock and examine the patient for burns and cuts or broken bones, which may have resulted from a fall after being hit. It's important that you give a lightning victim all the assistance you can, including getting him to professional medical attention. Take encouragement in the fact that most people involved in lightning mishaps make full recoveries.

Despite the danger of electrical storms, taking basic precautions will greatly reduce the hazard.

• Don't stay near a prominent object on the landscape, and don't allow yourself to become such an object.

• Avoid moisture when possible, and insulate yourself from the ground.

• Don't huddle together in a group.

• Whistle a happy tune, and remember that thunder itself is just a deafening noise.

Flash Floods and Rain Rises

Between 1960 and 1970, more than 850 people perished in flood waters, and flash flooding can occur almost anywhere in the U.S. One of the most devastating floods in recent years was the one in Colorado's Big Thompson Canyon. Yet, ironically, some of the most dangerous floods are those in the desert Southwest, where total annual rainfall is only about 10 inches. In these areas, June through September is the rainy period. Typically, clear mornings give way to cloudy afternoons that culminate in real cloud-rolling thunderstorms around 4 o'clock. The rains are often localized, perhaps drenching the area you're in while leaving things totally dry a mile away.

You don't have to be in the rainy area, though, to be threatened by flooding. Most desert soils are ill-equipped to absorb water quickly. So when torrential rains fall, the water simply collects in natural drainage systems. Small washes empty into larger ones, which flow into others. The volume of water grows until large washes, miles from a rainstorm, can be inundated with moving walls of water several feet high. Even when the rise is not spectacular, it can be dangerous.

One October in Utah's White Canyon, I hiked along a growing stream all day as the autumn rains continued to fall. That night we took the precaution of camping on a high knoll. By morning, the stream had grown to a roiling torrent, and our camp was completely isolated, with the river in front and towering cliffs behind. We were safe and quite content to watch the changing patterns of rainwater streak the limestone walls and observe the chocolate undulations of the river. But the scene was a potent reminder of the dangers of fast-rising water.

Hikers be aware of possible floods and stay out of washes and narrow canyons. Never try to cross a flowing wash; the turbid waters often conceal drop-offs or deep channels. If you happen to be heading for a route that is a river, like the Virgin River "Narrows" or the Escalante in Utah, plan the trip to avoid typically rainy periods.

Cyclists are not immune to the hazards of flash flooding. Roadways in both town and country can be turned into temporary aqueducts by drenching rains. This is no time for the bicyclist to try the two-pedal backstroke. Fast water, even when shallow, can throw you off balance or hide dangerous potholes. It's possible that whole sections of road may be washed out.

Tackling a rain-swollen river in a canoe can lead to a wet conclusion like this one.

More often, a road will be crossed by dry washes that become very *wet* washes during heavy rains. While driving near a dry lake bed in Texas, I saw water-depth markers, measuring from 1 to 5 feet, in every dip of the road. They seemed incongruous on that hot, dry day. Had I been cycling in the rain, however, you can bet I'd have had flash floods on my mind.

Rises in water due to rain are a mixed blessing for canoeists. As a kid, I bottom-bumped down the boulders of the Housatonic River in Connecticut one summer. My cousins and I were so hungry for white water that three times we reran the one set of decent rapids we were able to find. Our chants for rain and a water rise went unanswered. And by the time we were through, the bottom of the old wood-and-canvas canoe looked as though it had been danced on by a gorilla wearing golf shoes.

Although there are such times when an increase in water flow is prayed for, a river during flood stage can be an awesome and frightening display of energy. What normally might be an easy run in a canoe can be turned into a hydraulic nightmare. Reflex waves and suckholes may appear where before there were only ripples. Eddies that once offered a safe place to rest might be transformed into dangerous whirlpools. Navigating this kind of high water requires real expertise. Even then, it should be run only after you've scouted the full length of each rapid to be taken.

The danger of flood water was impressed upon me several springs ago when I was asked to help find a lost canoe on the Gallatin River. The stranger who requested my assistance gave me assurances that the river was low enough to be easily navigable, and so it seemed where we put in my canoe. After rounding a few bends, however, I knew we were in trouble. High water had uprooted whole clumps of swamp maples and even large cottonwoods, making the Gallatin a devilish obstacle course of log jams and bristling debris. It was only a matter of time before the canoe became a submarine. When it happened, the cold water took my breath away. I hung onto the stern painter until the swamped canoe came to a grating halt against a submerged tree.

Luckily, we suffered nothing worse than water-logged pride. Nearly a full day later—with the aid of chain saw and hand winch—we pulled my 17-footer from the river's grip. It was only then that I let the stranger know that he could paddle his *own* canoe down any future high river of his choice.

SECTION II

**Camping
in the Heat**

5

Hot Spots and Hot-Weather Clothes

The Okefenokee is a vast and primitive swamp stretching for hundreds of square miles across southeastern Georgia. It's a miasmic expanse choked with rotting vegetation that stains the water a deep brown. Here in the tangled madness of roots and tendrils lives a lushness of lizards, newts, toads, and snakes—slipping through the water, hanging from branches, crouching on logs and lily pads. The canebreak rattlesnake, the slimy salamander, the five-lined skink, the two-toed Amphiuma, the pig frog and the eastern cottonmouth are some of the more interesting inhabitants. Here, too, are strange plants with names like bladderwort and butterwort. Unable to get sufficient sustenance from the surrounding muck, they ensnare insects to consume their bodies for protein.

Death is commonplace in the Okefenokee. Alligators by the thousands lurk amidst the golden club and the yellow-eyed grass, devouring creatures that swim or slither too near. Snakes also attack fish, frogs, and mammals. And snapping turtles weighing up to 150 pounds are big enough to break a child's arm. More subtle but no less devastating is the quick death rendered by the flash of a swamp bird's beak.

Then there are the noises. The blood-chilling bellow of alligators thrashing in the redroots and the spike rushes. The ear-splitting din of the wart-covered oak toad and the barking tree frog. The birds, too.

In the heat, alligators lurk amidst golden and yellow-eyed grass.

The Okefenokee is not the only hot spot with a special kind of attraction. Most of the land east of the Rockies is hot and humid during the dog days of July and August. And there's certainly a lot of hiking, biking, and canoeing country in that expanse. There are also the hot, arid summers found in the western rain shadows—those areas that aren't quite deserts yet get little rain because clouds dump most of their moisture on the west slopes of nearby mountains. Even in high mountainous country across the U.S. there are days when the sun feels so hot it can make a bare head spin and a strong man feel like a wet sock.

For many people, however, it's the desert that is synonymous with heat.

Of the four distinct deserts in the U.S., the Great Basin Desert, covering much of Nevada and Utah, is the largest. It's a land of hot summers but cold winters, and it is characterized by sagebrush and saltbrush.

The Mohave, most notorious of the U.S. deserts, lies south of the Great Basin Desert. In July of 1913, a thermometer in the Mojave hit 134° F.—the highest temperature ever recorded in the U.S. This intensity of heat was unusual, of course. Normally, the daily high temperature for July averages only 116° F.

The Sonoran Desert, ranging over large parts of California and Arizona, is the lushest desert of the four because of its winter and summer rainfalls.

And finally there is the Chihuahuan Desert, spilling into the U.S. from Mexico and covering parts of New Mexico and Texas with spiny shrubs and cacti.

In total, these four deserts cover half a million square miles of backpacking, bicycling, and—yes—even canoeing possibilities.

The outdoor opportunities are there. So is the heat. It's a dilemma, especially if you're someone like me who begins to sweat as soon as snow leaves the ground. But man in general has a low tolerance for heat. Normal body temperature for a human is 98.6° F. and about all the body can survive is 107° F. Yet man, like plants and animals, can adapt himself to live comfortably even when the air is hot.

Theories on Keeping Cool

A major concern in this process of adaptation is what we wear or don't wear. There are two schools of thought about keeping cool.

The hike-naked-into-the-light theory says that the fewer the clothes, the cooler you'll be. The believers in this view are identified by a trail

Here various degrees of the take-it-off and the cover-it-up theories of keeping cool are displayed against a backcrop of The Needles, Canyonlands National Park.

wardrobe that consists of hiking boots, socks, shorts, and perhaps a halter top for the ladies; occasionally the shorts and halter seem optional.

Holding the opposite point of view is the cover-it-to-cool-it contingent. They wear long pants, long-sleeved shirts, and wide-brimmed hats.

As devoted as the advocates of these two schools seem, the objective evidence supports only one theory.

The facts show that the body is warmed in several different ways. Radiant heat from the sun is one way; heat from sunlight reflected off ground and water is another. We are also heated by convection when warm air currents come into contact with our skin and by conduction when we come into contact with hot surfaces.

Perhaps more to the point is the fact that a naked person walking in the desert sun experiences a bodily heat gain equal to the effect of a 10°F. rise in the air temperature.* So much for the go-naked-into-

* *The Deserts of the Southwest*, Peggy Larson, Sierra Club Books, 1977. p. 185.

the-light theory. It seems that the clothes have it. The right kind of clothing will help to shield the body from four kinds of heat: radiated, reflected, convected, and conducted.

But there's more to heat than just temperature. As the saying goes, "It's not the heat, it's the humidity." Dry air (air with low humidity) will evaporate sweat from your skin faster than will humid air. Consequently, evaporative cooling, your body's primary way of getting rid of excess heat, will be more effective when the humidity is low. A bike tour in Arizona at 90° F. can seem refreshing compared to a stifling hike in Maryland at the same temperature and 80 percent humidity.

Humidity or not, however, your clothes and your sweat are going to help keep you cool. In hot, dry climates, a layer of clothing over your skin keeps sweat from evaporating too fast to be effective. In hot, humid climates, when there's more sweat than can be evaporated quickly, clothes hold that moisture until it *can* be used for evaporative cooling, instead of letting it drip off.

But there's more to dressing for the heat than just hopping into anything that happens to be at hand. A look at the traditional desert dweller's clothing suggests several characteristics we might well incorporate into our own hot-weather dress. For centuries, nomads of the Sahara have worn loose-fitting garments, as have other Arabs whose typical dress consists of light-colored flowing robes.

The light colors effectively reflect solar rays instead of absorbing them. The looseness of fit allows for plenty of ventilation, which is needed to help evaporative cooling. Now, I grant that cultural biases would make most of us feel rather silly hiking down the trail in flowing robes. But light-colored, loose-fitting shirts and pants can easily form the basis of your hot-weather wardrobe without making you look and feel out of place.

Beyond these general clothing concerns, there are certain attributes of specific items of clothing that will make them more suitable for the heat and make you more adaptable in hot weather.

Clothes

Underwear

To some people, underwear seems superfluous when the temperature is on the rise. Others simply wear what they usually wear. This decision is usually fine for men. Cotton jockey-type shorts will feel cool when damp, even though they're close-fitting. Boxer-style shorts are looser fitting and so should provide more ventilation. I find, however, that boxer shorts creep and wad up during outdoor activity and generally make me feel as if I've stuffed a rag bag in my pants.

Gals have a different problem. Ladies' unders are usually made of synthetics, like nylon or rayon. These materials won't absorb moisture, so they end up feeling miserably clammy—not what you need on a stick day in Alabama. The alternatives are woman's cotton underwear or borrowed men's shorts.

Socks

Hikers have a tough time keeping their feet comfortable in the heat. Cyclists have wind to cool their heels; canoeists have water. Hikers have only the ground, and sometimes the ground temperature is considerably higher than that of the air. Ground surfaces reach 150° F. regularly in the desert. I also remember that the tar on the road to my childhood swimming hole in New England got too hot to walk on with bare feet.

Socks and boots act as insulators in these situations. Wool may seem like a strange choice for socks, but it can keep heat out as effectively as it keeps heat in. Wool can also absorb sweat and wick it away from your skin, as can "wick" socks and socks made of Olefin (see page 37). If you normally wear two pairs of socks when backpacking, don't switch to one pair just because it's hot. An improper fit would probably result, and that could easily lead to blisters.

Two pairs of socks are a must if you use lightweight inner socks made of polypropylene. Since polypro won't absorb moisture, you'll need an outer sock that will, or blisters will pop out on your feet like acne on a teenager's cheeks. For people with a one sock (for each foot) preference, there are now polypro/ wool combinations that have a inner layer of polypro to move moisture away from your feet to an outer layer of wool. It's the two socks in one principle. DuPont also makes a polyester called Coolmax for use in clothing, including socks. Their claim is that it wicks moisture away from your body at more than twice the rate of polypropylene.

It's important, in hot weather, to keep your socks clean. Only then will they remain resilient enough to both insulate and cushion your feet. Most biodegradable backpacking soaps that can be used on you and your dishes are mild enough to use on socks. Under extremely warm conditions, it may be wise to change socks two or three times a day. This tactic will probably mean washing socks on the trail, but it will be time well spent. Just turn wet socks inside out and lash them to the back of your pack, and they will dry in short order. During your sock-washing stops, your feet get some fresh air.

Changing frequently to fresh socks will go a long way toward keeping your feet happy on a hot trail.

That can only make them feel happier.

There are tales of pilots downed in the desert during World War II who, after walking for miles, took their boots off and were unable to get them back onto swollen feet. Some such stories undoubtedly are true, but few of us are going to hike for pleasure under such adverse conditions. A good airing and a dash of foot powder have always made my feet walk easier when the trail was shimmering ahead of me.

Boots

For canoeing or cycling, the regular lightweight shoes you would normally wear are quite suitable for the heat. At times, it will be tempting to go barefooted. However, severe sunburn may result. If the tender skin on top of your feet gets burned, you really won't want to put on your shoes.

For hikers, sandals and sneakers are tempting. Yet both conduct heat easily from the ground to your feet and offer no protection from the sharp spines in some types of vegetation. Most hikers have one pair of hiking boots, which they use in all backpacking situations. But if you're in the market for new boots and you expect to do a lot of hot-weather hiking, there are some features to avoid. A boot that has a fully padded interior will be too warm because it won't let your foot breathe adequately. Even partially padded interiors may make the boot uncomfortably hot. Also avoid boots that are higher than the top of your ankle.

One boot that may be inexpensive enough to buy as a second pair to be used just for hot weather, is the G. I. Tropical Combat boot. The lower part of the book is made of leather, and the rest is made of nylon and cotton canvas. Two metal vents at the instep help to cool your feet. The sole has lugs. A pair averages just a tad over 3 pounds. And if you cut these boots down to ankle height, they'll weigh even less. The combination of fabric uppers and canvas lining with no padding makes for a boot that breathes exceptionally well. You can get them at most Army-surplus outlets.

If you want to spend more, look to the boot revolution of the 80s that beefed up running shoes into hiking boots. There are now lots of leather/nylon combinations that provide much cooler walking than the traditional all-leather boot.

Insoles

Despite your careful selection of socks and boots, the right insoles can add even more ventilation. *Don't* get the foam-rubber variety; they are insufferably hot. But a woven type of insole allows more air than usual to move around your feet.

Pants

Even though the cover-up theory of keeping cool is the most effective in practice, many people—especially cyclists—are addicted to shorts. Legs that are well tanned to begin with can withstand exposure to sun better than can unseasoned legs. But no skin is immune to the sun's burning rays. Sun screens or sun blocks are recommended for use on any exposed skin (see page 125). By all means, take long pants whenever you'll be in the sun for long periods of time. You can wear the shorts for part of the day and then switch to more protection when the sun's at its highest.

Probably the most difficult thing about finding suitable pants, long or short, is finding ones that are loose enough. Blue jeans tend to be fairly restrictive, although they're probably worn more than anything else. Chinos are better because of their light color and their usually fuller cut. You can always buy pants a size larger than you normally wear and hold them up with a wide belt or a pair of suspenders.

As for material, cotton really comes into its own when the weather is hot. It absorbs moisture, unlike synthetics, so it can store sweat for evaporative cooling. And it also feels cool to the touch when it's wet. Some pants will not be 100 percent cotton. Even these can be suitable if they have a low percentage of synthetic fibers.

Shirts

Although it's usually easy to find shirts that are baggy enough, the questions of long or short sleeves and of proper material are similar to the questions posed about pants. The answers are the same. Long sleeves are the best, and you always have the choice of rolling them up. Cotton is probably more important in shirts than in pants because a shirt covers areas of your body that produce more sweat.

Hats

When given a choice, I go without a hat. But there is no choice under the blistering heat of a noonday sun. My thinning Turner pate (I'm told it comes from my mother's side of the family) will not allow it. I'd end up with a boiled brain and refried bacon for a scalp.

A hat is primarily for protection against the sun, so some kind of brim is useful. Canoeists can contend with an all-around brim, but a hiker using a contoured external-frame pack will find that any brim much wider than two inches will constantly collide with his packframe, knocking his hat maddeningly askew. One way around this is to perform major surgery on the hat brim in the back, while leaving the rest of it intact. Selecting a hat with a narrow brim is another choice. And fashioning your own hat along the lines of the French Foreign Legion design is also a possibility. Actually, a brim in the front and a cloth flap in the back and partially around the sides—to protect your ears—is an ideal solution for backpackers. A rig like this can be made easily enough by sewing or pinning a bandana to the back of something like a baseball cap.

Cyclists are faced with a different problem. The trick is to find a helmet that offers superior head protection, yet still keeps you cool. *Bicycling* magazine has given Bell's Quest Helmet top rating for its cooling ability. Another good choice is Performance's Aero Helmet. In any hot weather cycling helmet, look for air vents that are positioned to direct air over the top of your head. You'll also need a lot of sun block on your nose and neck.

No matter what kind of hat you wear, it should be equipped with something to hold it firmly in place. A lost hat under a hot sun can be more than inconvenient; it can be distinctly dangerous. A chin strap will be the answer on most kinds of hats with brims. You'll have to poke a couple of holes in the brim, one just in front of each ear. Then take a piece of cord or rawhide about three feet long, and push an end down through each of the holes. Pull the midsection of the cord snugly against the back of the hat's crown. You can either tie the strap under your chin or attach a sliding cord tightener. When you want to get the chin strap out of the way, just fasten it around the crown of the hat instead of under your chin.

That's it. Obviously your hot-weather wardrobe won't be extensive. But each item is important and serves a definite purpose. Lose your hat and you'll have to improvise with a bandana or some other item. Tear a hole in the back of your shirt and you'd better be prepared to sew it up. Because of their importance, make sure clothes and footwear are in top condition before you start any hot-weather trip.

6

Coping with the Heat

What Is Hot and Why

It was May. Several feet of snow still covered the grass in the front yard of our Montana home. That's why we had escaped to the south—southern Arizona, just above the Mexican border. This is country Father Kino once explored. He was responsible for pioneering a route from the present town of Lukeville to what has become the city of Yuma, considered the hottest metropolitan area in the country. Over the years, this route has killed so many travelers because of the heat and the lack of water that it was named the Devil's Highway. It was here that Linda and I decided to go backpacking.

The long whiplike wands of the ocotillo were in bloom, tipped with reds that startled the eye as they waved against the muted tones of volcanic rock and soil. Hedgehog, fishhook, and prickly-pear cacti abounded, along with the massive organ-pipe cactus and the ubiquitous teddy-bear chollas. It is a world of plants and animals that must adapt to the heat. I was well aware of that need to adapt as I trudged among the mesquite and catclaw with sweat rolling down my face. It was the only running water for miles. Even Linda's face seemed content to remain dry, as I stopped to suck down a long drink from my water bottle.

In the desert, plants, animals, and people learn to adjust to the heat or perish.

It's no secret that various people react differently to heat. I have some desert-rat friends who think nothing of going out to kick about in temperatures that push close to 100° F. My body starts to wilt when the temperature hits 80° F. It doesn't seem to make any difference whether it's the humid air of South Carolina's Swamp Fox Trail or the dry air of the Big Bend country in Texas.

Your reaction to heat depends on your individual metabolism and on your physical and climatic conditioning. Some people never do adjust to hot climates, but others adjust quickly. I find it interesting that people born in hot climates actually develop more sweat glands than those born in moderate or cold climates. But most of us can become acclimated somewhat to heat so that we can function with lower heart rate, blood pressure, and body temperature while increasing our sweat output.

The actual acclimation time is usually from two to seven days. The process should start with short periods of moderate exercise—two one-hour stints the first day—and build up gradually each day. Don't overdo the exercise since it will only slow down the acclimation process. Be sure to drink plenty of water during this time. The more physically fit you are to begin with, the faster you will acclimate.

Once you've adjusted your body to working in the heat, it should stay acclimated, without any further exercise, for about two weeks. But it's wise to get some exercise at least once a week to keep yourself in tune for coping with hot weather. Fortunately, acclimation in a hot, humid environment is transferable to a hot, dry climate, and the reverse is also true.

If you take the time to acclimate, however, don't think you are thereby immune to heat stress. It is important for you to be aware of the potential for heat stress whenever you'll exert yourself in hot weather.

One of the best ways to actually measure the probability of heat stress is to measure the air's capacity for evaporative cooling by using a wet-bulb thermometer. As its name suggests, this device consists of a thermometer with a wet muslin wick attached to the bulb. After the wick is dampened and given time to equalize with the surrounding temperature, the thermometer is twirled in the air by an attached handle. As the thermometer is spun, water evaporating from the wick will lower the temperature reading. Since more evaporation takes place in dry air than in humid air, the lower the wet-bulb reading, the less is the likelihood of heat stress.

Generally speaking, temperatures below 65° F. on a wet-bulb thermometer pose little danger of ill effects from heat. Between 66 and 70° F., you should be sure to drink plenty of water to replace what

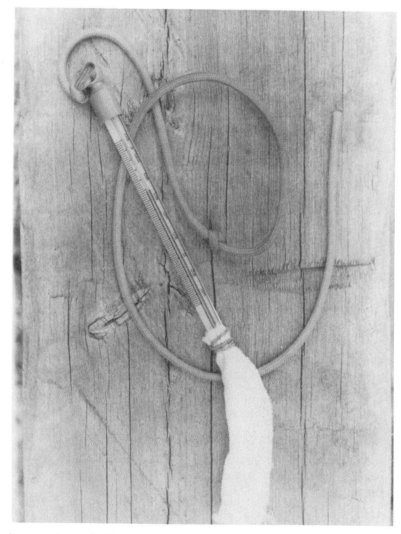

A homemade wet-bulb thermometer will help keep you aware of the heat-stress potential.

you'll lose from sweating. From 71 to 75° F. on a wet-bulb thermometer, you'll experience high heat stress. In addition to consuming lots of water, you should moderate your pace and take frequent rest stops. Above 76° F., the danger of heat stress is extreme. You'd be wise to sit in camp and quietly contemplate the wonders of photosynthesis.

Most self-propelled travelers, of course, will not lug around a regular wet-bulb thermometer. But you can fashion your own using a pocket thermometer. Simply attach a cotton wick (a strip cut from the neck band of an old T-shirt serves well) to the bulb with an elastic band. Then tie a string to the top of the thermometer. Dampen the wick, and spin the whole affair to get a wet-bulb reading. Do this before you hit the trail and periodically while you are on the trail. If the humidity is dangerously high, you can heed the message and take appropriate action.

Even off the trail, humid air has drawbacks for the camper. While dry air lets heat radiate quickly into the atmosphere at night, humid air tends to hold heat close to the earth. Thus, the desert is likely to give you noticeable relief from the heat after dark, but humid areas often will not.

Clouds have a similar moderating effect on temperature fluctuation but one that is independent of humidity. Clear days make for hotter temperatures because maximum radiation from the sun reaches the earth. Under cloudy skies, daytime temperatures are lower because radiation is inhibited. On the other hand, cloudy nights tend to be warmer than clear nights because less radiant heat is allowed to escape into the atmosphere.

Handling Heat on the Trail

The Dip Method

One way of keeping cool that some people believe should rank alongside the cover-it-to-cool-it method (see page 84) is the keep-it-wet method. Your body naturally keeps your skin moist by sweating. The sweat evaporates, and you're cooled. If, however, you provide some other form of external moisture, you can conserve your body's moisture and be ahead of the game.

Campers traveling wherever streams and ponds are frequent may find that periodic immersions *with* clothes on is the most effective way to combat oppressive heat. I recommend a clothed (instead of unclothed) dip not through any sense of modesty but simply for a longer-lasting cooling effect. Clothes retain moisture much longer than bare skin and so keep you cool longer. Even salt water will do for this purpose. The dried brine may feel a little sticky on your body and in your clothes, but that may be a small price for keeping cool.

As delightful as a plunge in a pool may be on a hot day, there are places where you should resist the temptation. The desert is one of those places. Water is usually very scarce, and the rare pool large enough for a body dunk might be the only drinking water for miles. For most people I know, filling their canteens with used bath water has never been very appealing.

Yet I must confess I once succumbed to the lure of a desert pool. I'd been hiking up dry washes and over limestone rimrocks for four days in Utah's canyon country. It was spring, but the air had been hot and was still hot when I hit the top of Salt Creek drainage. Down on the canyon floor flowed a trickle. As the miles trudged by, the trickle grew to a stream some six inches deep and four feet across. Most of the morning I was content to dip my water bottle and pour the cool water over myself. By the middle of the afternoon, things had changed. The stream was larger, and I was hotter. One dip certainly wouldn't contaminate so much water.

It was a deep transparent pool that finally lured me—a five-by-five pocket of cool water with a soft sandy bottom, surrounded by small plants of the deepest green. Suddenly, I was suspended in liquid luxury with my clothes in a heap on the sand. Somehow the place and the time demanded nakedness as a sort of tribute to the wildness that surrounded me—the overhanging canyon cliffs, the sand, the ancient cottonwood, the life-giving water, and the silence. Later I soaked my clothes and put them on and walked off into the sun feeling more refreshed than I had in years.

• *Sun Screen*—Such dunkings, as helpful as they may be to the cooling system and the spirit, tend to dilute any sun-screen lotion you may have smeared over crucial spots such as nose, neck, and back of hands. Reanoint these places after a dip to make sure you don't end up with crisp skin. The best sun screen or sun block, by the way, is one that contains PABA (Para-aminobenzoic acid). This is the most effective ingredient for keeping out the ultraviolet rays, which damage your skin. Remember that your eyes should be protected too, with shade or sunglasses or both. This is especially important when you're around sand or water (or snow), where reflected rays can increase the chance of sunblindness.

Pace and Rest Stops

Although water to dip in is always available for the canoeists, backpacking and bicycling frequently lead you through dry country where a slow pace and numerous rest stops are necessary. If there is one thing designed to keep you moving on a hot day, it's not moving at all for a while. Rest stops needn't be taken by the clock. I prefer to stop when my body tells me to, and that's well before I'm really tired or thirsty.

Stopping is much more enjoyable when you aren't so exhausted that all you can do is lie prostrate and pant. In fact, both lying down and panting can be counterproductive in hot weather. Rocks and sand exposed to the sun can be 30 to 50° F. hotter than is the air temperature several feet off the ground. In 1972, National Park Service personnel recorded a ground temperature of 201° F. in Death Valley.

When you sit or lie on any superheated surface, your body will absorb heat readily. So it's important, when you're resting, to sit in shade. A tarp or tent fly can be used when no natural shade is available. The sparse vegetation of a desert may not afford much shade, but there's usually enough around from which to string a sun awning. Sometimes you can simply throw a tarp over a bush or string it from your bicycle to produce a patch of shade big enough for your needs.

As for panting, you can lose up to a quart of water a day through respiration. Keeping your mouth closed will minimize this loss and help keep your mouth and lips from drying out. You can also use some sort of lip balm for additional protection.

Rest stops should not be just passive affairs; while you're resting you should be actively involved in keeping yourself in traveling trim. There are some strange theories about how to rest on the trail. Many of them are filled with DON'TS. "Don't take off your pack." "Don't take off your boots." "Don't drink water." Well, don't listen to any of that. Of course, take off your pack. (And that pack had better be one of the external-frame kind if you expect your back to get any benefit of evaporative cooling. Non-frame and internal-frame packs that nestle right up against your body are intolerably hot.) Take off your boots and socks, too. Your feet will appreciate a good airing. If you can manage a foot bath and a change into clean socks, so much the better.

As for drinking water, you'd better have some if you want to keep going (see Chapter 7). You may want to add something like Gatorade or Gookinaid E.R.G. to your water. These mixes don't reduce your need for water. But because of the balance of minerals and sugar in them, they allow rapid absorption of the water. The minerals replace those you lose in your own sweat, especially salt. And the sugar—usually glucose, which can be taken directly into your blood stream without being digested—supplies you with energy. Some of the other really sugary drinks, on the other hand, can cause temporary dehydration by drawing water into your stomach and away from the other parts of your body.

A note of warning: whenever water is scarce be sure the cap is screwed tightly on your water container before you set it down. A quart of water seeping into the soil doesn't help your body.

Avoiding the Hottest Part of the Day

Really hot days may require you to halt any travel during the warmest part of the day. It's during such conditions that you may have to revise your normal sleeping-waking schedule.

Early morning is the coolest part of the day. The sun is low in the sky, and the earth has lost some of the heat it absorbed from the sun the previous day. Although the sun will be low in the evening too, the earth will still be holding a great deal of absorbed heat. At any rate, both morning and evening provide some relief from a high sun, and they often have the added benefit of unabashedly gaudy sunrises and

Recreational Equipment Inc.
A rest stop is a time for drinking water.

In a forest that has a sparse overstory, like this pine forest in Florida, hiking can be done by moonlight as well as by day.

sunsets. In clear, dry air, the colors are usually spectacular in their contrast. Humid air softens and blends the colors into a more subtle show.

Traveling at Night

The most neglected time for travel is the nighttime. Traveling by moonlight can be an enchanting experience and worth doing even when the air temperature isn't unbearably hot. Light from the moon has a cool quality that seems to impart to objects their own luminescence. Of course, different areas have varying intensities of moonlight.

Desert areas, characterized by scant vegetation, will have high nighttime visibility because light from the moon and stars is unobstructed. Heavy forested areas like Maine or Minnesota tend to be dark along wooded trails, although forests of pine like those found along Florida's Ocala Trail often let in enough light to allow night hiking during the full moon without the use of artificial light. Roadways and water ways usually provide unobstructed light from the moon for cycling and canoeing. More than once I've sat in camp at night watching with fascination as a canoe disappeared in a distant reflection of moonlight.

Traveling in relative darkness is another matter. Sometimes it's possible to continue without artificial light when you're walking or paddling in wide-open areas. But when you're hiking or biking in areas with nearby vegetation, some additional light will be needed.

• *Flashlight or Headlamp*—For normal use around camp, a flashlight is fine. But for extended night travel in the dark, a headlamp is necessary. This kind of unit has an elastic headband to which a light is attached. A separate battery case is attached to you belt. While you're using these systems, your hands are free. The Recreational Equipment, Inc., headlamp has two separate lenses and lamps. The 0.15-amp lamp operates up to 17 hours on lithium batteries; the 0.3-amp lamp will get you over 8 hours of light. REI also has a Waterproof Headlamp that's a good choice for canoeing. If you tip over, the headlamp is waterproof down to a depth of 30 feet. Scary.

Some people swear by carbide headlamps. Such a lamp slowly produces acetylene gas by dripping water on calcium carbide. The gas is burned. I grant that the light cast by these lamps is quite agreeable. But these little gadgets are temperamental and require too much attention and extra paraphernalia to make them very attractive for me to carry. I prefer battery-powered lights.

Battery-powered headlamp systems are especially helpful for the cyclist because the beam can be directed easily to the exact area needed. This ability becomes extremely important in warning motorists you're there.

But even with a headlamp you may find it difficult to avoid tire-deflating thorns and spines that desert country tends to spew along its roadways. Where this is a real problem, cyclists should probably use "clincher' type tires with thornproof inner tubes. They're heavy, but they'll save you the tedious repair time you'd spend on the vulnerable "sew-up" type of tire.

Even mountain bikes with their more durable tires and thorn resistant butyl tubes might need the added protection of something like Mr. Tuffy MTB Tube Protectors. Put these between the tube and tire for off-road cycling in thorny country.

A small light strapped to your leg is helpful in warning motorists of your whereabouts.

Another light that is extremely useful for the cyclists is the little French unit intended to be strapped to your leg. It doesn't offer you light to see by, but its up-and-down movement warns motorists of your whereabouts. If you're a cyclist, you should also use plenty of reflective tape on your bike and even your clothing to make sure you're highly visible to people driving along the highway. Performance has what they call the Victory Jacket. It could be a life saver. The Scotchlite Brand reflective finish on this garment is visible in the beam of a headlight for up to 600 feet.

• *Batteries*—Standard carbon-zinc batteries have a very short shelf life when exposed to heat, so avoid them. During extended use, such as nighttime travel, alkaline batteries have up to five times the life of carbon-zinc cells. But lithium batteries are the best. One cell will put out 2.8 volts as compared to the 1.5 volts of the other cells. The lithium cell has a constant output rate, and one "D" size cell weighs under 3 ounces and has the same light hours as alkaline cells weighing 18 ounces.

Lithium batteries come in "D" and "C" sizes. The "D" size will last 24 hours. When a lithium battery is used in conventional flashlights or headlamps that require two conventional batteries, a dummy cell must be included in order to fill space and complete the circuit. Lithium cells seem to be expensive. Yet they're actually cheaper than alkaline batteries when you figure the light-hours delivered.

• *Bulbs*—For extended use with "D" alkaline batteries, I'd use a PR 6 bulb. Use a PR 4 if you're using "C" cells. With one lithium "D" size battery, you should use a #14 bulb, but take plenty of spares. Since each bulb has only four hours of life, you'll need six bulbs to go the 24-hour life of the battery. A PR 15 bulb should be used with two "D" size lithium batteries. The combined cells will have a life of 13 hours, and the bulb will go 11 hours, so one spare should be enough.

• *Navigation*—Your ability to travel at night, of course, depends on your grasp of what lies beyond the beam of your headlamp. In a lot of arid country, trails don't exist; the soil and rocks won't hold them. Night travel in such places should be confined to periods that have enough natural light for you to distinguish landmarks and rock markers or cairns that may be used to indicate a route. In a real pinch, you can get your general bearings from the North Star (the one pointed at by the two end starts of the Big Dipper's bowl). But the North Star will hardly enable you to pinpoint your position or tell you where you ought to travel in the immediate surroundings. When in doubt, it's better to cope with the heat of daylight hours than to get lost in the cool of the night.

Certainly, the possibilities of getting lost in hot places aren't limited to night travel. One memorable challenge in keeping track of myself occurred on a blistering day in the Great Basin Desert. It was the middle of a five-day cross-country trek, and I'd been hiking for miles up a dry wash with map in hand. The towering rock labyrinths on either side of the constantly narrowing wash were reduced to an intricate hodgepodge of contour lines on my 1-inch-to-the-mile map. It was only by following each bend in the wash with its miniature counterpart on the map that I could tell where I was.

There were dozens of hidden side canyons, and I wanted to be sure to find the one that would lead into a place a friend had affectionately dubbed Starvation Pocket. With the use of my sweat-impregnated map, I did locate the spot and immediately renamed it Satan's Stove. There wasn't a wisp of air in that cup of crisp weeds. Heat bounced off the sandstone walls and sent us scurrying for a low cleft in the rocks that offered a patch of shade.

It wasn't until late afternoon that we dared venture out to climb over the high rim and drop into another drainage. The navigating would have posed no problems once over that rim into the next canyon, but the clear trickle of water beckoning from the shade of a cottonwood compelled us to make that first stretch of canyon bottom camp for the night. Relief from the heat was more important to us than was covering more ground.

In Camp

Selecting a Campsite

Be it dry or humid, the first concern in selecting a hot-weather campsite is shade, unless you'll be in camp only when the sun is down. In some locations, the shade may be only what you can make with a tarp or a tent. However, it is often possible to find the natural shade of a forest, a lone tree, or a rock outcropping. Take advantage of these naturally protected spots, keeping in mind that the shadows will shift considerably between the time you set up camp and when you get up in the morning. If you want to sleep late, make sure your bed is positioned to avoid the morning sun. In a hot climate, even a low sun can drive you from your nest.

A well-placed tarp will provide shade even when the shifting shadows of nearby trees will not.

Wind is another concern in selecting a hot-weather campsite. In humid locations you may well want the wind's cooling effects. If so, position your camp on a knoll or other exposed area where you'll receive its full benifit.

When you're in a dry climate, the wind may be too potent an evaporative force. In this case, a natural or makeshift windbreak can be used to protect your living space. By using your ingenuity, you can pitch a tarp to provide protection against both wind and sun.

Water is an important commodity to have near your camp. You don't, however, want water *in* your camp. Desert locales, especially, are abundant with dry washes and other natural drainage areas that can quickly become inundated during a rain. Avoid such spots even though there isn't a cloud in the sky.

Fire vs. Stove

Any kind of unnecessary heat is the last thing you want when the temperature is soaring. Yet most of the food you carry on a trip will require cooking. Should you depend on a fire or a stove?

A fire makes most sense in a situation where you'll have to carry most of your own water supply. Canoeists are the exception here; they can carry from home many gallons of water without being overburdened. And they can always treat and drink the water they're floating on. But when you're cycling or hiking in arid country, you'll have to haul extra water on your back or your bike. That means a great deal of extra weight. You may very well decide to leave your stove and fuel at home and resign yourself to sweating a bit over a cooking fire.

Before you make a final choice, however, find out whether fires are allowed and whether ample firewood is available where you'll be traveling. Many national parks, monuments, and forests prohibit open fires or the gathering of firewood. Other places may ban fires during dry seasons, which often coincide with hot weather.

Even where no such prohibitions are in force, fuel may be very scarce. Although the woody skeletons of cacti and other plants are usually quite flammable when dry, they can remain surprisingly water logged after a rain. Humid locations tend to offer more productive picking for wood. But even those places can produce soggy wood that may make you settle for a dinner of cold cardboard gruel when it should have been chicken and noodles.

One basic concern with any fire is that it must not make a mess of the surroundings. Piles of blackened rocks surrounded by compacted, bare ground are hardly a part of the natural environment. In fact, they can go a long way toward turning the backcountry into a slum.

The first thing to remember is that you don't need rocks to make an efficient and safe fire. You can make a good fireplace that will disappear after you've gone by digging one into the ground.

I prefer to carry a cookstove when I'm not overburdened with water. Stoves are more efficient than a fire and cooler to cook over. Stoves do, though, deserve some special attention when used in hot weather. Self-pressurized stoves, like the Svea and the Optimus 8R, must be warmed in order to operate efficiently. Yet they can build up too much pressure from excess heat. This problem will cause the safety valve to release, shooting out fuel that is invariably ignited by the burner flame.

A stove "blow-out" of this sort is usually caused when the stove is surrounded too closely with a wind screen or when an extra-large pot is put on the burner. In either case, heat is reflected back onto the stove, causing overheating.

If a "blow-out" does happen, let it continue for 20 or 30 seconds. This may be enough time to relieve the pressure and allow the safety release to shut itself off. Otherwise, it's important to extinguish the flame before the rubber parts of the safety valve start to char.

One method used by a friend of mine who consistently goes out in the most inferno-like weather is to douse the thing with water, which he does as a matter of routine. Another method, which shows more bravado involves diving in, turning off the burner, and then blowing out the flame as it shoots from the safety valve. The process is rather like Red Adair capping a runaway oil well. I've seen it used, but I've never elected to use this technique myself.

No matter how you put out the conflagration, check the safety valve to see that the rubber gasket is still pliable and not crusty. It's wise to carry a spare tank lid (the safety valve is in this) and gasket in case either one needs replacing.

Stoves using butane cartridges operate differently from self-pressurized models. Butane cartridges are *not* intended to get warm. Excess heat can make them rupture, spewing flames in all directions. Be very careful to avoid surrounding these stoves with a wind screen or a large pot when the air temperature is high.

The safest stove to use in hot weather is one that must be pumped to provide fuel pressure.

Food

The whole purpose of a stove or a fire is to cook your food. You certainly don't want to watch the flames or warm your feet when the mercury is in the 80s. Yet the thought of food is often unappetizing in hot weather when you're exerting yourself. Fats, in particular, are unpalatable. I remember one exceptionally hot summer when I worked on a construction crew in New England. At noon my sandwiches inspired little interest, but I'd easily down a quart of juice or water. I lost 20 pounds in ten weeks during that hot spell.

An important aspect of food is that it requires water for digestion. Water holds products of digestion in solution so that they can pass through the intestine walls into your bloodstream. It's also needed to carry waste materials from your body. So in order to conserve your body's water while you're on the trail, it's better to eat small amounts of food frequently than to eat a big meal at one sitting.

Dehydrated and freeze-dried foods are staples of hikers and bikers because they're so light. But they do need water to rehydrate, and some require a lot. In many hot-weather situations, that means additional water weight that you'll have to carry. So the temptation is to carry canned foods, but they are also heavy. Perhaps the important thing to remember when making your decision between the two kinds of foods is that much of the water used to rehydrate freeze-dried and dehydrated foods is used by your body to replace water you've lost during exercise. In other words, the extra water you carry to rehydrate dehydrated food serves two purposes which canned foods may not.

Tent, Tarp, or Open Air?

Several considerations go into your selection of a shelter or your decision to use no shelter at all. If there is a reasonable likelihood of rain, you'll want at the least a tarp. Are biting bugs or other creatures such as snakes, spiders, or scorpions a real concern? A floored tent may be the only answer, even if the creatures are more imaginary than real. Crawlies that creep through your head are just as sleep robbing as those that actually are in your camp. When conditions permit, however, a bed that's open to the sky can provide a star show that will mesmerize you into sleep faster than any flock of sheep.

• *Tents*—Many tents are oppressive in hot weather because they're too small or don't provide enough ventilation or both. When you're constantly rolling into another warm body, a hot night can be made miserable, even if the body is one you usually love.

Kelty has a tent called the Windfoil Breeze that sports see-through "no-see-um" proof walls. There's plenty of ventilation, and the 110 x 57 inch floor space is ample.

The tent will effectively keep out bugs and other creepie crawlies. But when rain starts, you'll have to dash out and put on the rain fly.

Another hot-weather tent comes from the Moss Tent Works. The Star Gazer is a roomy (5'8" x 7'1") free-standing, two-man tent. Its unique feature is a netted window in the top, which allows you to gaze at the stars while you're lying in bed. More important in hot weather, the window serves as a chimney to produce a continuous flow of air for good ventilation. When the rain fly is on, it covers the top window, but some ventilation is still maintained.

Recreational Equipment, Inc.

Even in the heat, a floored tent may be the only answer to imaginary creepy crawlies.

• *Tarps*—Tarps can be pitched in numerous configurations to protect you against sun, wind, and rain. Avoid dark-colored models that will absorb heat. You can fashion your own tarp using a sheet of .004-inch plastic. Don't get clear or black plastic. A translucent piece of white Visqueen is your best bet. Use pebbles or Vis-Clamps to secure guy lines where necessary.

• *Hammocks*—Often overlooked is the possibility of using a hammock in hot weather. One can be used wherever suitable props are available to hold it off the ground. A regular version will elevate you above the heat of the ground and the nocturnal things that crawl about there. It will also surround your body with air. A breeze on the backside can be quite welcome in the middle of a muggy night. Although a regular hammock won't keep out the sun, rain, and bugs, there is a special hammock that will. Campmor offers the Heavy Duty Jungle Insect Proof Hammock (phew) with a 38 x 79 inch sleeping space that is covered by a rainfly. Unfortunately, it has a water-proof bottom which means no breeze for the backside. But it will keep the rain out and still provide for ventilation without bugs.

The most satisfactory sleeping arrangement in many hot-weather situations may be a sleeping pad beneath, an old sheet above, and a pack for a pillow.

Bedding

Whether you sleep with or without a shelter, your needs in bedding can be quite variable even in hot climates. Sizzling daytime temperatures aren't necessarily followed by hot nights, particularly in the desert. It's wise to find out about average day and night temperatures before you decide what you'll sleep in. Nighttime temperatures in Arizona in July may call for a sleeping bag, while Massachusetts during that month might require only a sheet.

• *Sleeping Bags*—A light down or polyester bag will be all you'll need in most areas where warm days turn into cool nights. Even sleeping bag liners or covers may provide sufficient comfort, while cutting down on weight.

• *Sheets*—A sheet isn't typical camping fare, yet I've happily used one while hiking in New England, Florida, and Georgia. I've found it best to leave the whiter-than-white numbers in the linen closet where they won't show the dirt. An old brown sheet from an Army-surplus sleeping bag suits my needs perfectly. Lacking one of these, you can use any dark-colored sheet you can sneak out of the house.

• *Sleeping Pads*—You'll want to use an open-cell pad with a cover on it, since closed-cell pads will not absorb moisture and therefore will become uncomfortably hot. In areas that are both hot and moist, the pad's cover should consist of waterproof material on the bottom and breathable material on the top. This combination will prevent ground water from getting in but also allow sweat to be absorbed by the pad so it won't feel hot. From time to time, you'll want to remove the cover so both it and the pad can get a good airing. In dry climates, a completely breathable cover will allow the pad to dry without your removing the cover.

Sleeping

Sleeping in the heat is not always uninterrupted. You may find yourself awakened at midnight by a long thirst (you'll be inundated with the importance of water, in the next chapter), a night sound, or the refreshing hint of a breeze. Whatever the reason for waking, make yourself get up for a few minutes to savor the night air. Dew has a way of liberating sweet earthy smells. Listen for the nocturnal sound of frogs and birds. Search the darkness or the moonlight for the texture of the muted landscape. Let your senses take something of the evening's ambiance back to bed with you. You'll sleep more peacefully.

7

Water, Water

The names read like titles of surrealistic paintings: Island in the Sky, The Needles, Land of Standing Rock, The Devil's Kitchen, Upheaval Dome, Paul Bunyon's Potty. But these weren't the works of Salvador Dali. They were landmarks on a map covering 400 square miles of fantastically eroded sandstone—Canyonlands National Park in southeastern Utah.

At the heart of this ongoing process of erosion are the Green and the Colorado Rivers, whose churning waters have gnawed into the rocks for millions of years to form twisting canyons half a mile deep. Although I would always be within striking distance of those rivers, my main concern on that trip would be finding water.

The spring season had been unusually dry, and the ranger at Squaw Flat told us that most of the intermittent streams held nothing more than dust. We carried 1½ gallons of water each, but the circle trip we had planned through the backcountry depended on locating water along the way.

As immense and dry as that land is, it has a special fascination. The country engulfs you in rocks—shades of white, black, orange, and rust are carved into an infinite array of pillars, arches, walls, and domes, as if nature had gone somewhat mad. The subtleties are there too. The sandstone is softened by tenacious desert flowers that pull their color

111

The arid canyon country of the Great Basin Desert engulfs you with sandstone pillars, domes, and ledges. Notice person silhouetted in opening at bottom.

from moisture deep in the sand. Lichen and gnarled piñon, a glimpse of a mule deer, and the high wail of coyotes on the night wind all remind you of the variety of life there.

We reached a place called Chesler Park on our second day. It's a parched meadow surrounded on three sides by walls of rock. In the south wall, a tight notch leads down into a crazy jumble of boulders, chutes, and vertical drops. There are no trails here. We had to go by instinct, squeezing through rock passages with packs scraping the sides, only to meet sheer rock walls that forced us to try other corridors. Route finding was a matter of feeling our way through this labyrinth. Topo maps were useless. Sometimes we had to remove our packs and go underground. The rocks would close in, leaving only a low tunnel through which we'd crawl fifty to sixty feet before seeing daylight.

After hours of such scrambling, we broke out onto a long shelf overlooking a boulder-strewn meadow bordered by sandstone pillars. Finding water was a must. If we couldn't locate any by evening, we'd have to backtrack next morning up through the rock maze.

The stream bed leading out of the low end of the meadow turned up nothing. Potholes in the rocks were as dry as chalk. It was only when we sought the shade of a low ledge that we stumbled on a protected pocket of rock that had collected rain water as it seeped down through a crack in the overhang. Finding that isolated source of water made the difference between picking our way back to the car and being able to continue through the intriguing and remote backcountry of Canyonlands. In short, it was absolutely essential to the successful completion of our trip.

But arid country isn't the only place where water is a major concern for campers. Many moist areas of the U.S. may be abundant with water, yet most of these sources are contaminated by waste products or natural pathogens. Even in wilderness areas of the northern Rockies, a microorganism called Giardia lamblia, which is carried by beaver and other warm-blooded animals, can cause stomach cramps and diarrhea. Consequently, campers are faced with either scarce water or water of questionable purity.

The Importance of Water

Nevertheless, water is indispensable, and in hot weather you need more than usual. As discussed previously (see page 84), sweat helps cool your body through evaporation. Just how effectively this process works can be demonstrated by putting a filled water bag—the kind that "sweats"—and a filled canteen in the sun. A thermometer will show that when the water in the canteen exceeds 100° F., the water in the "sweating" water bag will still be in the 70s. Your body is cooled in the same way. But the water your body loses in the form of sweat must be replaced. Otherwise you'll start to dehydrate and overheat.

Although about two thirds of your body is composed of water, most of that is needed for your circulatory system. The inner core of your body is kept cool when heat is transferred to your blood, which then is pumped to surface areas of your skin. There the heat can radiate to the air. But if body water lost through sweat is not replaced, water is taken from your blood, making it thicker and reducing its volume.

This means more work for your heart. It also means that your blood circulation is slowed considerably, causing a dangerous temperature rise in your body's core. Research has shown that it's possible to lose one quart of water an hour while hiking in really hot weather. If your body is down two quarts of water and that water isn't replaced, your body loses 25 percent efficiency. Besides, the mere act of hiking when the thermometer gets up around 110° F. decreases your efficiency another 25 percent. When you combine these two factors, you're functioning at only half your possible efficiency.

Dehydration causes other problems. Even before your body becomes 5 percent dehydrated, you'll begin to feel uncomfortable effects. You'll be thirsty and lose your appetite. You'll also feel sleepy. Your temperature will rise, and you may get sick to your stomach. Between 6 and 10 percent dehydration, the discomforts heighten. Symptoms include a dry mouth, difficulty in talking, dizziness, a headache, and labored breathing. You may also feel a tingling in your arms and legs; your skin may get a blue tint, and you may be unable to walk. Obviously, you're in trouble. If air temperature reaches the 90s and body dehydration reaches 15 percent, you're probably dead.

How Much Water?

As dangerous as dehydration can be, drinking enough water to replace what's been lost will quickly restore your efficiency, provided you haven't lost more than about 10 percent of your body weight. The experience of two U.S. aviators during World War II dramatizes this fact.* After escaping from the Germans in Italy, the airmen hid in an

---

* Recounted in *Afoot in the Desert*, publication of Environmental Information Division, U.S.A.F., Maxwell Air Force Base, Alabama

attic to avoid recapture. For six days they survived on one pint of water before falling out of the loft from weakness. They finally managed to drag themselves over to water. And after drinking three pints each, they were able to walk and could even feel the energy returning to their bodies.

The camper with a bit of foresight will not find himself in quite such a position. The need for plenty of water still remains, however. Just how much water should be consumed is a question that's been raised for years. There was a time when coaches, trainers, and others who dealt with athletes preached the gospel of abstinence. The belief was that water in the stomach made you logy and inefficient on the court or the playing field. It wasn't until World War II that extensive research was done on the water needs of, and the effects of heat on, active people. Dr. E.F. Adolph, then at the University of Rochester, led the research, the findings of which are still used today. They can be found in the book *Physiology of Man in the Desert*, E.F. Adolph and Associates, 1947.

One thing that Adolph found out about water is that abstinence does *not* make the body work better. Though it's true that large amounts of water, especially cold water, will tend to slow you down, frequent sips of water are needed to keep your body running smoothly whenever you're sweating.

The most obvious signal of our need for water is thirst. Unfortunately, like a warning light on the dashboard of your car, it doesn't appear until you are already low. The result is that you have a tendency to replenish your supply only at meals, when drinking fluids seems to come naturally. So you may be somewhat dehydrated between meals unless you make a conscious effort to drink water while you're on the trail.

Profuse sweating is often a secondary indication that your body's water needs replenishing. Just the sight of sweat dripping from your nose may send you scrambling for the water bottle. Yet sweat is most obvious in humid weather, when it doesn't evaporate quickly from your skin and clothing.

In dry air, however, the amount of water loss is deceptive. Sweat can evaporate so quickly that it is imperceptible on your skin. So when exerting yourself in dry air, you'll have to drink water even when you may not think it's necessary.

The exact amount of water you, as an individual, will need in hot weather depends on many factors. Among them are air temperature, humidity, amount of shade available, amount of exercise, your physical conditioning, and your metabolism.

The quantity that's usually suggested is one gallon per person per

The only way to re-place the fluids your body loses through sweating is to drink water, and plenty of it.

day. But this may be too much or too little for you, depending on the specific situation. Use one gallon as a base amount only.

To estimate your own needs more precisely, it's wise to keep some records of your water consumption under varying conditions. Also write down the dry-bulb and wet-bulb (see page 94) temperatures, along with how far you travel in sun or shade and over what kind of terrain. By comparing this data with the amount of water you use for drinking and cooking each day, you'll get to the point where you can estimate your water needs very closely. Always remember, however, to figure in some extra for an emergency.

Whether or not you must carry your complete water supply will make a great difference in trip planning and logistics. One gallon of water weighs 8¼ pounds. That adds up to around 16½ pounds, in addition to your other gear, for a 48-hour trip through totally dry country. Those water pounds put a real crimp in the number of days you can plan to hike or bike in parched surroundings. And remember: when your water supply is a little *less* than half gone, your trip had better be half over.

Water Containers

All that water must, of course, be carried in something. At the start of a trip or whenever you find a watering hole, you can use your stomach as a water container without the ill effects that were once believed to occur. By drinking as much as a quart of water, even if you don't feel thirsty, you'll have the benefit of that much more water that doesn't have to be carried in your pack.

For the greater part of your supply, though, you need reliable water containers. Weight, bulk, and durability are all concerns. On first consideration, the lightest containers may seem best, but beware of flimsy ones that might puncture or crack easily. This doesn't mean you should avoid all plastic models. I've used the same polyethylene bottles for years, and they're very satisfactory. Because they're opaque, I can tell at a glance how full they are, and the quart sizes allow me to distribute my water load in various pockets and corners of my pack. Larger containers are rather unwieldy. They also cause a sizable loss of your water supply if one springs a leak.

I've found that a wide-mouthed bottle is the easiest kind to fill from seeps and other hard-to-reach water sources. Consequently, I carry at least one wide-mouthed bottle for retrieving water. An important feature on any water bottle or canteen is a top that is attached to the container. Losing a cap may seem unlikely, but there's no sense in taking chances in areas where water is so crucial.

Plastic bottles aren't the only possibilities for light, durable containers. Wineskins are quite effective, despite the rather restricted neck opening, which makes filling one a chore. Wineskins are light and have the added benefit of being collapsible when empty, a quality that facilitates stuffing them into small spaces to get them out of the way. FasTrak Systems, Inc. sells something called the Camelbak for cyclists. Its 40-ounce plastic water bag straps to your back, and a hose is looped through your helmet strap with a bite valve positioned near your mouth so you can sip while cycling. There are insulated models for hot weather use.

Whatever kind of containers you use, it's wise to label them clearly with the word WATER, if there's any chance of their being confused with something else, such as stove fuel. A friend of mine once settled into an old mine shack for what he thought would be a quiet night before taking off on a three-day hike. After putting some potatoes on the stove to simmer, he settled down in the other room to read. The explosion that wracked the shack unsettled dust that hadn't stirred in years. It also set the dingy curtains on fire and spattered bits of potato into every corner of the kitchen. The "water" he'd been using to cook the spuds was in fact white gas. To this day I always admire the bright, bold lettering that's been added to all of Norm's containers.

When carrying water in hot weather, you may want to keep bottles or wineskins wrapped in clothing in the middle of your pack. It will be more difficult to get a drink this way. But when you do, it won't be the temperature of bath water. Cloth-covered containers. on the other hand, should be kept dampened and should be hung outside your pack.

Before storing water containers for any length of time, wash them out with soap and water and then with baking soda to prevent any bacteria or funky smells from developing. Leave container tops off so air can circulate inside.

Finding Water

Not every hot-weather trip will require you to carry all your water. Often you'll be able to locate more than enough to supply your needs and will have to carry only a quart bottle for the occasional dry stretch. Then there are times, like my Canyonlands adventure, when completion of a trip depends on finding water even though you aren't sure you'll find it. In these situations, you've got to know where to look and what to look for.

The use of a topographic map my seem like a logical starting place, and in many locations it may be. Maps of arid regions, however, have a tendency to show springs, streams, and even lakes that are only intermittent. At certain times of year these spots may be valuable water sources; at other times, they may offer nothing but sand. The only way to check on the state of such watering holes is to talk with people who have had very recent first-hand experience at the spots. This is not always easy or possible in places that get little traffic.

In many dry areas, even in remote country, stock tanks or ponds are provided by ranchers to water their herds. These may not be indicated on topo maps. But local people may know of them, or a windmill may mark their location. The presence of cattle or sheep suggests that water is available somewhere in the area. If you follow these animals or their tracks, you'll probably find the source.

Wildlife can also provide clues to water. I've followed game trails in many parts of the country that have led to springs and seeps where I could fill my canteens. Once in desert country, I noticed deer tracks funneling into the mouth of a side canyon that was not a part of my planned route. Nevertheless, I decided to take a half hour off to investigate. Within fifteen minutes, I'd found a large pool at the base of a sandstone escarpment. The spot was so appealing that it became home for the night. Camped a fair distance from the pool, I was able

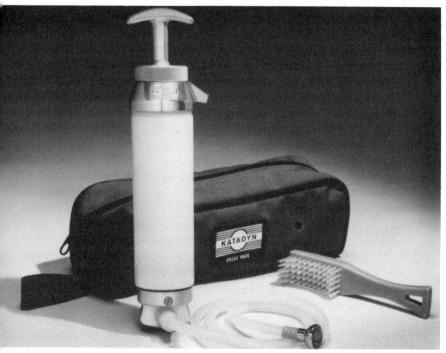

Katadyn U.S.A.
Katadyn Pocket Water Filter for purifying untreated water in the field.

to watch mule deer come in for water at twilight. It was a memorable place that I'd have missed had I not taken the time to follow those tracks.

In rocky country, the most productive place to look for water is in potholes. The rock most likely to hold water is limestone. It is soluble, and water eats it away to form pockets and caves, where water may be stored. Sandstone and lava are also likely rocks in which to find water. Potholes in these formations provide natural leakproof containers for collecting rain water. Yet these holes aren't always visible; they can be hidden under outcroppings or on top of ledges. Often you must poke around a lot to find them. Also look at the base of cliffs and canyon walls for possible seeps and springs.

Large rocks and boulders in a dry stream bed can hide water holes, too. When the stream is flowing, it undermines rocks on their down-stream sides, forming deep holes. These holes often hold water long after the rest of the stream is dry. Look, also, in the rocks along the undercut banks on the outside bends of stream beds.

Digging for water may seem like a long shot, but it is a possibility. Wherever you find saturated soil, there's a chance of hitting water after digging a bit. Most likely it will be muddy, but you can let suspended particles settle and then pour off the clear water. In all but emergency situations, it makes little sense to dig unless there is a definite sign of ground water. Green vegetation in an otherwise dry landscape, especially if it occurs on a hillside, suggests a spring or seep that may flow just beneath the surface of the ground. Cottonwood and sycamores are good indicators of ground water near the surface, while something like mesquite, which has deep root systems, is not.

Strangely enough, rain is an obvious source of uncontaminated water that often goes overlooked. Summer thunderstorms along the east coast and in the southwest can fill all your empty water containers if you can collect it in a tarp or poncho and funnel it into your bottles. When you're in camp you can even suspend a tarp to form a dish-like reservoir where gallons of fresh water can be caught.

A final possibility is the use of water caches. A cache is a place to hide gear or provisions for future use. When you expect a long, dry stretch on your route, it is often possible to set up a water cache before the start of your trip. The precaution of *hiding* water and other provisions in arid country is more than a matter of romantic paranoia. There are those of our species who would gladly help themselves to water and other goodies without considering the consequences to those who left them there. So to be on the safe side, it is wise to bury your supplies when possible. Then draw a detailed map to insure that you can find the cache later. Glass water jugs are best for storing water underground. There's always the possibility that an inquisitive rodent might chew through a plastic container. A variation on the use of a cache is to have someone meet you with fresh supplies at a designated place and time. The importance of working out specific directions for this kind of resupply should be obvious.

Purifying Water

Finding water is one concern. Finding *pure* water is quite another matter. Nowadays it is more the exception than the rule to find potable water in lakes and streams. Contamination from animal, chemical, and human waste is likely in all but the most remote areas. Even there, microorganisms spawned in the wilderness itself can cause problems.

To be completely safe, all water that doesn't come from a guaranteed pure source should be treated. Failure to do so might result in an

Even in the wilderness, water can be contaminated by microorganisms.
GRUMMAN BOATS.

upset stomach or diarrhea, which can be a potent dehydrating force. Severe illness can even be caused by impure water. So if there is any question, as there almost always is, take the time to treat your supply.

Boiling water is a standard method of purification. But somehow the process is not very appealing when mirages shimmer in the distance and sweat rolls in hot beads down your front. Still it remains an option and can always be used should you get caught without other means of purifying your water. Boiling should be continued for 10 minutes at sea level. But since the boiling point of water decreases one degree centigrade for every 1000-foot gain in elevation, water will have to be boiled longer as you gain altitude. Fifteen minutes at 5000 feet and twenty minutes at 8000 feet is sufficient.

One system that formerly was standard for treating water is chlorination. Either Halazone tablets containing chlorine or a small amount of either Chlorox or Purex was added to a full canteen of water and left to stand for thirty minutes. The problem with this method is that it will not neutralize contamination caused by organic matter.

Considering that drawback, iodination seems the best answer.* The use of iodine along with some form of filtration should remove or neutralize any pathogens in your water supply. Currently, there are three iodine treatments in common use.

• One of the simplest methods is to carry a vial of 2 percent tincture of iodine. Eight drops of this solution added to a quart of water results in disinfected water that tastes strongly of iodine. Besides, some people also get a queasy feeling about dumping into their water a substance made for putting on cuts.

• To disguise the fact that you are putting iodine in your water, you can use Globatine tablets (tetraglycine hydroperiodide) instead. These can be bought under the brand name Potable Aqua® tablets. One tablet per quart of water is the usual dosage. Unfortunately, these tablets lose their effectiveness when exposed to high temperatures and also when exposed to air for more than short periods of time.

• The third possibility is to make your own iodine-treatment kit. You'll need a one-ounce *glass* bottle with a tight-fitting cap. To this bottle add 6 grams of USP grade resublimed iodine crystals (I_2), which you can get from a druggist. Fill the bottle with water; cap it, and shake it for a minute or so. It is the iodine solution, *not the crystals,* that you'll want to use for purification purposes.

---

* The discussion of iodine treatments is adapted from information presented in "Son of Iodine. Out of Halazone," C.B. McCartan, *Wilderness Camping,* Vol. 8, No. 4; and "A Simple, Safe Method of Water Purification for Backpackers," Fredrick H. Kahn and Barbara R. Visscher, *Backpacker,* #26.

Let the crystals settle, and then put 5 capfuls of the *solution* into one quart or one liter of water. This assumes the cap holds 2½ cubic centimeter—standard on a one-ounce bottle. It also assumes that the water temperature is about 70°F.

After the solution has been in the water for 15 minutes, the water is usually ready to drink.

Highly contaminated water, however, should be exposed to the iodine solution for a longer period—up to an hour. You must add more at colder temperatures. (At water temperatures near freezing, eight caps of the solution should be added to a quart of water, and it should stand for up to an hour before it's used.)

When you run out of solution in your one-ounce bottle, simply refill it with water and shake. The crystals will remain effective for years, provided you cover them with water when they're stored and keep the cap screwed securely on the bottle.

There are a few precautions to take when using iodination as a water treatment.

• First, never treat water with iodine while it is in an aluminum container. Long exposure of iodine to aluminum can cause dangerous reactions. This does not mean iodinized water can't be drunk from aluminum cups or used to cook in aluminum pots and plates. Short-term exposure is not dangerous, provided the utensils are washed afterwards.

• Second, the ascorbic acid present in drink mixes like Wyler's lemonade can reduce the effectiveness of iodine tablets and solutions. Do not add mixes with ascorbic acid to your water until *after* the iodine has had a chance to do its job.

• Finally, if you are pregnant or have hyperthyroidism, don't use iodine treatments in your water unless you first consult a physician.

The most reliable, and expensive, purifying system is one that uses a microfiltration process to remove all harmful bacteria, fungi, cysts, and parasites. Katadyn U.S.A. Inc. has the Katadyn Pocket Filter that's about the size of a two-cell flashlight and will process a quart of water in a minute.

Water that has a lot of foreign material in it should be poured through a T-shirt or bandana to remove large particles before treatment and filtration. Muddy water should be left to settle before you pour the clearer water into another container and treat it.

Water is one of your most important considerations while traveling in hot weather. The newest equipment and best camping know-how is useless without it. An old Maya saying puts it succinctly:

Drink, drink while there is water.

8

Hot-Weather Hazards

The history of desert country is filled with stories of miraculous survival in the face of overwhelming odds. One such episode happened in the southwestern part of Arizona back in 1905, and it involved a scrappy fellow by the name of Pablo Valencia.*

It seems Pablo rode his horse into the desert with only one day's supply of water. As bad luck would have it, he remained out there for eight days. Before he was discovered by a certain Dr. W.J. McGee, Valencia had ridden thirty-five miles and walked or crawled well over one hundred miles. During that time the temperature ranged between 80° F. and 103° F., and Pablo had to claw his way back to water in the heat of the sun. When he was found by Dr. McGee, he had lost 25 percent of his body weight, and his blood was so thick from dehydration that his open wounds did not bleed until he was given water.

Pablo Valencia survived. According to medical science, he shouldn't have.

If we pay attention to proper preparation, sensible planning, and a good supply of water, few of us will ever face the kind of harrowing predicament Valencia found himself in. However, anyone who ven-

---

* Recounted in *Afoot in the Desert*, publication of Environmental Information Division. U.S.A.F., Maxwell Air Force Base. Alabama

-tures out in hot weather, be it the dry southwest or the humid east, should know how to cope with injuries and illnesses related to sun and heat.

Sunburn

Most of us remember a time when the first warm days of summer have tempted us to peel down to the bare essentials and go about unburdened by layers of clothes. The white skin of winter soon turned pink, and by evening we were red-hot and repenting our overexposure.

Your skin can acclimate to the sun's rays to a certain extent, but it takes gradual breaking in. With unseasoned skin, start with only 15 minutes of exposure the first day and increase the time by 10 minutes each subsequent day. Even after you've become well tanned, midmorning to mid-afternoon is the time to be especially careful.

If you'll go about uncovered, you should use a good sun screen or block. PABA (Para aminobenzoic acid) is the effective ingredient in most of these preparations. Some people are allergic to it, so test a small amount on your skin for 15 to 30 minutes before covering yourself with it. Sweating and swimming will dilute and wash off these lotions. It's best to reapply them at regular intervals.

In certain situations, the potential burning effects of the sun can be underestimated. Probably the most dangerous time is a cloudy day when the intensity of the sun isn't apparent but when the ultraviolet rays are still coming through the overcast. A few years ago a friend of mine received uncomfortable burns on the tops of his feet while hiking barefooted on a cloudy day along a Mexican beach. He was fortunate only in that it was his last day before driving back to the U.S. His feet were so painful he had to drive without shoes.

Other times for special care against the sun's burning powers include those periods when you're surrounded by sand, rock, water, or snow. Canoeists are particularly susceptible to the reflected light that these surroundings can produce. In addition, high altitudes are subject to more intense rays from the sun than are low elevations, so be careful of sunburn when you're in the mountains.

But what do you do when you haven't been careful enough? Immersion in cold water is the most effective relief. And stay out of the sun. Cold-water compresses are an alternative where water is scarce. A spray such as Sunburn Cooler may relieve the pain somewhat. For the headache that may accompany prolonged exposure to the sun, take aspirin.

For severe sunburn where blisters develop, *do not* break the blisters or put on any antiseptic. Use only cold water—not ice water—to relieve the pain. And cover the area with clean clothing to act as a bandage until professional medical attention can be reached.

Sunblindness

Wherever the reflective glare of sunlight is great—such as on or near water, sand, and snow—"sunblindness" is a possibility. People afflicted with this injury don't always lose their sight, and if they do it is usually temporary. But impaired vision, a burning sensation, watery or dry eyes, and severe headache may be the more common symptoms of eye exposure to intense light over a prolonged period.

Injury is caused when ultraviolet rays burn the cornea of the eye. Less harmful is the muscle tension brought on by constant squinting.

Could it be that this canny canine knows something a lot of two-legged outdoor travelers ignore? Give your eyes a break with sunglasses to protect them from dangerous glare.

The prevention for these problems is eye protection by sun glasses. Dark-colored lenses are the best. When glare is extreme, the glasses should have side protection too. High-quality glasses, like Ray-Ban, will filter out most harmful rays and reduce harsh glare.

If sunblindness should occur, cold compresses placed over the eyes may offer relief. Aspirin will reduce muscle tension and headache. It is also extremely important to keep your eyes protected from further glare after you've had even a slight case of sunblindness.

Heat Cramps

Sweating is your body's primary way of cooling off. As you sweat, however, salt is lost from your body. If this salt is not replaced, an imbalance is caused that can produce cramps in your legs and abdomen. These cramps may occur even though plenty of water is being consumed. To prevent this problem, you should increase your salt intake whenever you're sweating a great deal. Simply salting your food more heavily than usual is often sufficient to replace salt that you've lost during hot weather. Adding mixes like Gatorade or Gookinaid to your drinking water also helps replace lost salt.

Salt tablets, commonly used in the past, are not recommended in most situations today. Current opinion suggests avoiding tablets in all but extreme conditions since they can cause nausea, stomachaches, and even vomiting, which may cause dehydration. When you're losing so much salt that tablets are necessary, take only those that are treated to dissolve in your intestines instead of your stomach. These will help avoid the unpleasant side effects.

If cramps do occur, press or massage the muscles to relieve the pain. Then sip salted water. Put a teaspoon of salt in a glass of water, and drink about half a glass every fifteen minutes for an hour. With rest and the salt solution, you should be in shape to continue after an hour or two. But keep up the high salt intake, by putting plenty of salt on your food, for the remainder of the trip.

Heat Exhaustion

Your body, as a secondary means of cooling, uses the circulatory system to carry heat from its core to surface areas, where the heat can radiate into the air. But when the weather gets really hot and you're pushing yourself, blood rushing from the body's core to the skin's surface can deprive vital organs of their needed blood supply and cause faintness and even collapse—a condition called heat exhaustion. A similar reaction can occur when dehydration causes reduced blood flow.

Heat exhaustion (and heat stroke) can usually be avoided by drinking plenty of water, taking extra salt, and avoiding strenuous exercise when the air is really hot. In very high humidity and air temperatures, however, heat exhaustion is always a possibility.

Heat cramps are often, but not always, a first sign of the gradual build-up toward heat exhaustion. Unexplained irritability is also a warning sign. So if you find yourself snapping at your companions for no apparent reason, it's time to slow down and consume plenty of water and salt.

The symptoms of full-fledged heat exhaustion include profuse sweating but a pale complexion. The victim may experience headache, lightheadedness, nausea, and—sometimes—vomiting. Extreme weakness and collapse are possible, but even then the victim's temperature will remain about the normal 98.6° F.

To treat heat exhaustion, get the patient out of the sun, lay him down on his back, and elevate his feet slightly. Loosen his clothing to promote better circulation. Use water or damp compresses to cool him off. Fanning will help too, but you must be careful not to chill the patient. Every half-hour for an hour, have him drink a glass of water with a teaspoon of salt dissolved in it. However, if vomiting results, stop this treatment. You will probably want to make camp as soon as possible. After a good night's rest, the patient should be able to continue at a slow pace in the morning.

Heat Stroke

Of all the heat-related illnesses, heat stroke is the most dangerous. The condition can be fatal, and it calls for immediate action. Heat stroke comes on suddenly and is caused by a breakdown of the body's primary cooling mechanism, resulting in massive overheating. Elderly people and those who are over weight or out of shape are most susceptible to it. The most revealing symptom after collapse and possible loss of consciousness is flushed, hot skin but *no sweating*. The victim's pulse will be very rapid and strong, and his temperature will be very high, possibly 105° to 106° F. If he is conscious, he may be irrational or complain of a splitting headache.

Treatment must begin immediately and consist of cooling off the patient as quickly as possible. Get him in the shade and remove his clothes. If immersion in cool water is possible, do it without hesitation.

Otherwise, sponge him with water or alcohol and fan him. Once his pulse rate has dropped below 110 beats a minute, stop the cooling measures, but keep a careful watch to make sure overheating doesn't set in again. You can rub the patient's body to encourage blood circulation when his temperature has come down below 102° F., but do not give him any stimulants. After the patient's condition has been stabilized, keep him quiet and arrange his evacuation to medical supervision.

Note: People who have suffered from heat stroke must be very careful about going out in the sun or heat for several months or more afterwards.

Heat stroke, of course, is an extreme reaction to the environment. It's something you should know about and be prepared to treat. Yet there is little likelihood of your being afflicted with it, if you follow the advice presented in this section. The use of proper clothing and pacing, along with careful attention to adequate water and salt intake, should keep you hotfooting it down the trail right into winter.

SECTION III

Camping
in the Cold

9

Cold-Weather Clothes

Many hikers who look with benevolence on backpacking during the balmy months cast a jaundiced eye on hiking in the snow. Winter, for such people, is the time for fireside musings and for viewing slides of last July's hike in the Green Mountains. Hiking when it's cold is bad enough, they say, but if you go out in the cold *and* snow, on purpose, to hike, you have reached the outer edge of sanity, looked over, and plunged into the frosty abyss.

This kind of skepticism was certainly in my mind when I started off on my first extended cross-country ski trip with a couple of experienced cold-weather campers. The trip started near a downhill ski area. As I plodded through the snow, I was convinced, that the skiers being whisked up the lifts were finding the day eminently more enjoyable than I was.

Yet as the sights and sounds of lift lines and congested slopes receded, some startling new perspectives invaded my clearing senses. We had climbed above all the clatter, and the silence that set in was immense. Packed slopes had given way to vast stretches of untracked powder. Contoured snow cornices along the ridge and inflated shapes of snow-covered pines took the edge off our voices and the scenery, making the world seem muffled and intimate, even though mountains stretched to the horizon.

Skiing far from ski lifts and the clamor of crowds can be addictive, especially when the powder is light and the air is crisp.

At 9,000 feet, we dug a snowcave and saw the sun turn the snow pink and then purple. Later, watching dinner simmer over the low hiss of the cook stove, I found myself inexplicably content to be sitting comfortably on a remote mountain in a house made of snow. Before settling into the enveloping warmth of my sleeping bag, I went outside to watch the rising moon turn the terrain into mile upon mile of translucent snow sculptures.

I knew then I had looked over the edge and taken the plunge.

Revelling in the frosty abyss, however, no matter how intriguing it seems, does require some special attention to your body's thermostat. For most of us, 98.6° F. is the normal body temperature. Too many degrees above that and your system starts to malfunction and short circuit, as I mentioned in the previous chapter. Your body can also get into trouble when its temperature drops more than a few degrees below normal (see Hypothermia, Chapter 4).

There are only two ways your system can produce heat:

• Food supplies fuel for your body's heat-producing machinery—its furnace. It is appropriate to think of your body as *burning* calories because calories express the heat or energy-producing value in the foods you consume.

• Exercise also produces heat. At the same time, exercise increases the number of calories your body must burn in order to keep you going.

When the weather is cold, your body must conserve heat. As the inner core of your body begins to cool, the flow of blood is restricted to skin surfaces, thus making more heat available to your vital organs. In addition, the circulation of blood to your extremities can be greatly reduced by your body as a way to conserve heat. That's why your hands and feet can get cold in the winter if you aren't careful.

While your body is working to conserve heat during cold weather, the weather itself has various ways of trying to take the heat away.

Even if your body restricts the flow of blood to skin surfaces, some heat does get there and a certain amount is lost through *radiation,* especially when your skin is exposed to the elements.

Conduction is another heat robber. Sitting directly on snow and ice or handling cold objects conducts heat away from your skin. And just being surrounded by cold air will do the same thing.

But *convection* is the primary stealer of heat. Wind will blow heat away from unprotected skin amazingly fast.

The odds in this tug of war for your body's heat are on the side of the elements, unless you can do something to aid your body. That aid is the use of insulation. Ironically, heat loss through radiation and conduction serves to warm a thin layer of air that surrounds and tends to cling to your body. Ideally, this buffer zone of warm air between your skin and the colder air of the atmosphere would act as an insulator to prevent you from losing heat faster than your body could produce it. Unfortunately, when your skin is left exposed, this thin layer of warm insulating air is constantly being removed by convection and being replaced by cool air. To prevent this heat-loss process from continuing, man invented clothes. Clothes cover the skin and trap still, warm air so it won't be blown away.

In theory, anything that traps air and holds it could be used to conserve your body heat. (Remember, clothes don't produce heat; only your body can do that.) Popcorn, straw, animal fur, or bird feathers should all work equally well as insulators. In practice, they don't. Why? Because some qualities besides dead air spaces are important.

For one thing, you'll carry your insulation on your body or in a pack, so it should be as light as possible. It should also fluff up, or loft, well in order to provide as thick a layer of dead air spaces as possible. Yet it should also be greatly compressible so that you can cram it into a small space when it's not in use. For comfort, the insulation should have a soft feel, and it should drape closely around the contours of your body to effectively hold warm air close and still. Finally, since convection is a prime cooling agent, the outer layer of any insulation should be impervious to wind.

Many materials fall far short of ideal. Popcorn and straw, for example, don't get very far at all. And by the time all factors are considered, only a handful of materials are left as effective insulators.

Before examining specific kinds of insulation, however, we should consider the problem of water. Moisture and wind are the evils of the winter-camping world. Wet clothing can conduct heat away from your body very rapidly. In addition, the evaporation of moisture from skin and insulation has a further cooling effect. So dampness, whether from sweat, rain, or snow, should be avoided.

The traditional way to avoid moisture from sweat is to wear several light layers of clothing so you can effectively control body temperature and hold sweating to a minimum. When you're working hard, you can trim down to one or two layers. Standing around camp, you can add more layers of shirts and sweaters to provide sufficient insulation. Realistically, though, you'll do some amount of sweating no matter how hard you try not to. Cold as it may be, I do a fair amount of dripping; I'm just built that way. To combat this inevitable moisture, the usual procedure is to use insulation that is breathable. Theoretically, this quality allows moisture to escape through your clothes instead of being trapped inside where it would quickly conduct heat away from your body. In fact, this system does cause some cooling by evaporation and conduction.

To circumvent this problem, a new approach for controlling moisture was devised by Jack Stephenson of Warmlite back in the 1950s. Actually, according to Jack, he got the idea from an old book on camping, which was published in the 30s. Called the vapor-barrier principle, this approach is based on the fact that your skin needs a micro-environment with a humidity content in the range of 70 percent to 90 percent.

In order to maintain this degree of humidity, particularly in cold, dry air, your body is continuously producing an unnoticeable amount of sweat, in the form of water *vapor*, which is just enough to prevent your skin from drying and cracking. The vapor-barrier principle reduces the need for this unnoticeable sweat by trapping vapor close to the skin with a waterproof, non-breathable layer of clothing. Because the layer is close to the skin, it is heated and condensation is prevented. Over the vapor barrier, regular layers of insulation are placed. A waterproof shell is used to keep moisture from entering from the outside.

The advantages of this system are many. Sweat of the noticeable kind— i.e., liquid water instead of water vapor—is *immediately* noticeable inside a vapor barrier because it isn't absorbed into the breathable insulation, and you can feel its presence right away. Consequently you can control this kind of sweating by removing layers of insulation or by increasing ventilation. The sweating that does occur does not get into outer insulation from the inside, and dampness from rain or snow is kept out with the waterproof shell. So your insulation stays completely dry and therefore much more effective than it would be otherwise, since conductive and evaporative cooling are eliminated.

Despite these advantages, the vapor barrier approach to coping with the cold never really came into wide-spread use in the 80s. Part of the problem is that most people don't understand the principle behind it, and, therefore pass it off as much hog-wash. Others may have tried the approach and found it uncomfortably clammy. In practice, the use of a vapor barrier does require some getting used to and some futzing with. Here are some suggestions:

—Don't use a vapor barrier unless it is quite cold, in the teens or below.
—*Before* you increase activity levels, take off outer layers of insulation to prevent sweat accumulation.
—Wear a light, close-fitting pair of polypropylene underwear next to your skin to prevent the clammy feeling you may get with coated ripstop nylon vapor barrier shirts or pants. Or try Warmlite's vapor barrier shirts/pants

made of what they call "*SOFT FUZZY* stuff." It feels like its name, and it doesn't make you feel like a stewed prune, although it does lock in moisture. —The layers that you wear over a vapor barrier (and a VB can be used under socks and mittens as well as under parka and pants) should be those recommended for any good layering system. However, you probably won't need as many layers with a VB.

Recreational Equipment Inc.

Polypropylene and polyester underwear moves moisture away from your skin to prevent evaporative cooling.

A Look at the Layers

Underwear

The virtues of wool and polypropylene fishnet underwear have been extolled sufficiently in Chapters 2 and 5. I'll just summarize by saying that the holes in these unders act as efficient dead air spaces when they're closely covered but then quickly convert to ventilation holes when they're uncovered. That combination is at the heart of a good cold-weather insulation system.

But the main purpose of the newer lightweight, tight-fitting polypropylene and polyester underwear is to move moisture away from your skin so you won't be cooled as it evaporates. This type of underwear offers only a small amount of insulation. But when it is used with outer layers of insulation that absorb moisture and move it away from your body, it becomes your first line of defense against cold.

Vapor Barrier

If you are going to take advantage of what a vapor barrier offers, you'll probably find it most comfortable over polypropylene underwear, for reasons I've already mentioned.

Turtleneck (Zip Front)

I've found a light wool turtleneck with a zipper going partway down the front is a good layer to go over any underwear. The close fit of the shirt makes for efficient utilization of the unders, while the high neck offers protection where it's needed. Both the neck and the head are parts of your body that are always receiving full supplies of blood in order to keep your brain functioning properly. Consequently, a tremendous amount of heat can be lost from an exposed neck or head. The zip-front turtleneck offers warmth when it's needed but can also be unzipped to offer fast cooling when you start to overheat.

Jacket and Sweater

Originally, the heading above this paragraph read "Wool Shirt and Sweater." And I haven't given up on wool as a sensible choice in a cold weather layering system. Pile, however has definitely come into its own as the first choice in cold weather insulation. Made of polyester (or nylon or acrylic) that has been "napped" into fluffy, spongy fabric, pile (and its relatives, bunting and fleece) is very durable. And since the fibers themselves absorb almost no moisture, the fabric can be wrung out after getting soaked, and it will provide almost optimum insulating efficiency while any remaining moisture quickly dries from the fabric's weave.

Pants

Wool pants are an answer in winter for the same reason I recommend wool shirts and sweaters. Long pants tend to be warmer than knickers, but the difference isn't appreciable. To protect your wool pants against getting really wet when you're involved in digging a snow cave, for example, you should take along a pair of light, waterproof outer pants or chaps. These can also be used as wind pants. Down-filled or polyester-filled bivouac pants are items for an expedition, but some winter campers do carry a pair of the polyester "warm-up" pants used by alpine skiers. Pile pants, like pile jackets have become popular, but they definitely need a breathable waterproof shell over them to keep snow from balling up on the fabric.

Insulated Parka (Jacket, Sweater, Vest)

In recent years, great bulky parkas filled with down or polyester have become popular in many areas. While these may be suitable for walking around town or campus, they are something less than desirable for most cold-weather situations. The problem is that they are too efficient. When you're sitting on a cold stump watching the moon come up through the pines, a big engulfing parka will feel great, no doubt. But when you're on the trail with a full pack, it will make you feel like a chicken in a hot pot. A further problem is that such a jacket tends to be an all-or-nothing-at-all affair. You either wear the whole roasty thing or you don't. Unzipping is a way to some temperature control, but not enough.

I'm not saying that insulated parkas have no place in cold weather. A lightweight model may be used effectively in combination with other layers of clothing. In extremely cold conditions, even a heavy parka may be desirable. But these big, puffy numbers are generally expedition-type garments, and K2 is not on our trip list in this book.

The pros and cons of down and polyester for use as insulation are discussed in Chapter 3. The main drawback of down is still its loss of insulative value when wet. But down can be used extremely effectively in a vapor-barrier system where it is sandwiched between two waterproof layers. However, when a parka will be exposed to dampness from either sweat or snow, a synthetic insulating material that absorbs almost no moisture is preferable.

Polyester fibers have attained a permanent place in clothing as well as in sleeping bags. The major difference between the three most widely used brands of fibers—DuPont's Hollofil II and Quallofil, and Fiber Industries' PolarGuard—is their length. Hollofil II and Quallofil, are so called staple-fibers and average two inches in length. PolarGuard, a continuous-filament fiber, is about 100 inches long. Continuous-filament polyester is more popular among most sleeping-bag manufacturers because they believe it is inherently more durable where large expanses of fabric and fiber occur between seams. Because the distance between seams is smaller in clothing, the advantage of a continuous fiber is minimized. Some clothing manufacturers prefer DuPont's Hollofil II and Quallofil because they have a silicone finish and, consequently a softer feel than PolarGuard.

Traditionally, the standard measure of insulative value has been thickness. Practically speaking, construction, moisture content, and other variables will influence the thermal resistance of clothing. But according to the traditional view, one inch of down, polyester, fiber-pile, or wool all have the save value of insulation. Well, the 3M Company claims that its introduction, in 1978, of Thinsulate Thermal Insulation makes the old theory obsolete. According to 3M, the more surface area there is in an insulative material, the more effectively it hold air still by means of surface friction. Therefore, says 3M, the smaller the fibers in an insulation, the more of them you can fit into a given space and the greater will be the surface area to hold air sill. This new theory seems to make sense, and it could drastically reduce the bulk, if not the weight, of future cold-weather clothing.

Thinsulate itself consists of extremely fine-fibers—finer than human hair—which are made of polyolefin. The 3M people claim this insulation provides almost twice the insulative value of an equal thickness of down, polyester, wool, or pile. Although Thinsulate is heavier than down, down must be stabilized between baffles. Since the baffles require the use of more material in a down garment, they thus minimize down's initial weight advantage. I have yet to try a parka filled with Thinsulate, but I've gotten unbiased reports that the insulation lives up to its manufacturer's claims and that it is very durable.

The newest wrinkle from 3M is their Thinsulate Ceramic insulation introduced in 1990. Here's what they say about it. And I quote directly from their handouts to give you an example of how modern technology has gotten into outdoor gear, and to give you a sense of how difficult it sometimes is to separate sales hype from honest performance reports:

"Thinsulate Ceramic insulation is composed of polyolefin and polyester fibers. Some of the polyester fibers contain ceramic particles having a structure which allows them to absorb more solar radiation than normal polyester fibers.

After absorbing the increased amounts of solar radiation, the ceramic containing fibers re-radiate the energy in the infrared red or heat energy band. This re-radiated energy is absorbed by the bulk of the insulation batt, which results in less heat loss from a human body. Any of the heat energy which is not absorbed by the insulation and penetrates the body will also cause an increase in body warmth.

Additionally, the ceramic containing fibers will absorb radiation heat loss from the body and re-radiate it back to the body or some of it may be re-absorbed by the insulation batt.

Tests with various fibers show that the exterior surface temperature of Thinsulate Ceramic insulation increases by several degrees when exposed to sunlight. This effect causes the 100 gram ceramic containing Thinsulate insulation to have up to a 25% greater effective clo than the same weight Thinsulate insulation without the ceramic containing fibers."

OOOkay. What do *you* think? Maybe it's time to go on to some talk of construction.

No matter what the fill, the most efficient parkas, in theory, have no or few sewn-through seams, which could create cold spots. Such construction, however, is expensive and is usually found only in expedition-type parkas. In practice, sewn-through and quilted construction, when worn under a parka shell, is sufficiently effective in all but the most severe cold-weather situations.

The types of fabrics used in parkas and vests vary. Nylon is often used because it's tough and light. Both ripstop and taffeta weaves are used in nylon shells and liners. Rip-stop has a thicker thread woven into the fabric at quarter-inch intervals. This feature increases the material's tear strength. Taffeta, on the other hand, has a continuous weave. As light as these fabrics are, any nylon material used in a garment should weigh at least 1.9 ounces a square yard in order to assure durability.

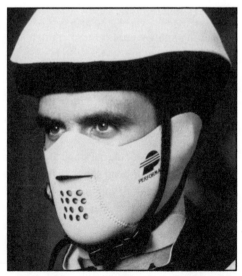

Cyclists have a unique problem of protecting their faces against windburn and frostbite.

Performance Bike Shop, 800-PBS-BIKE

Breathable waterproof material used in an insulated parka shell eliminates the need for a separate outer layer that's resistant to water and wind. It also makes down much more effective in damp, cold weather. Remember, though, that some moisture will still get into the down from the inside unless a vapor barrier is used between it and your skin.

When you're shopping for a parka, there are some special features to look for. A collar that will stand up against your neck with plenty of insulation in it is a good defense against heat loss. If an optional, detachable hood is available for the parka, get it. It may not be the best hood on the market, but worn over a wood hat and covered with a windbreaker hood, it can make you just about blizzard-proof.

Your parka should be on the long side. You'll be thankful for some extra insulation over your backside. A drawcord at the waist and bottom hem will also help keep the roaring winds from funneling up from beneath. There are other special features like hand-warming pockets and stormflaps over zippers, but they aren't all that important unless you plan to wear the parka as your outermost layer. If you can, however, get a parka with as much adjustable ventilation as possible.

Parka Shell

The last layer of your insulation system should be waterproof. Rain parkas are covered in detail in Chapter 2, and they are suitable for winter use. Perhaps I should reemphasize that the typical 60/40 parka is *not* waterproof. That fact was brought home to me recently when I was cross-country skiing in Yellowstone National Park. I'd taken along a 60/40 parka thinking that any falling snow would be cold enough to come off my clothing without much melting. A mid-February chinook ended that idea, and wet snow clung to my parka like burrs, soaking completely through by the end of the day. I'm convinced, at this point, that a breathable waterproof parka is the best way to fly in rain or snow.

Hat

As I've mentioned, the neck and the head are very vulnerable to heat loss. For this reason your head should have several lines of defense against the cold. The hood of both your parka shell and of your insulated parka (if you wear one) will form the outer layers. The inner layer should be wool or pile. If you can't stand the itch of wool on your head, at least use orlon. The best hat you can use is more like a head stocking with a hole for your face. This unlikely affair is called a balaclava, and it handily covers all of your head— except eyes, nose and mouth—and most of your neck. When all this protection is not needed, you can roll the balaclava up from the bottom and wear it like a stocking cap. A watch cap or a stocking cap that can be pulled over the nape of your neck may also be used. It's good insurance to take one of these in addition to a balaclava. The loss of a hat, if it's your only one, can mean real trouble.

Mitten and Gloves

Your hands and feet are difficult to keep warm because the flow of blood is reduced to these areas when your body core starts getting chilled. So, it's especially important to have good insulation for your hands and feet. To start with, in weather where there is any chance of frostbite, I wear an inner pair of silk gloves. They are extremely light, take up almost no room, and give some protection to your hands when you must perform some fussy, unmittened task like operating a camera or zipping up your pants.

Over these thin gloves I almost always use mittens since they are far more effective in conserving heat than gloves are. Inside a pair of mittens, all your fingers can huddle together for warmth, and a cold thumb can duck in occasionally to be surrounded by warm fingers. Wool mittens with a long-wristed outer liner of breathable waterproof make a good combination. The Austrian Dachstein mitt is made of a very tightly woven and preshrunk

Northern Outfitters

Silk glove liners will provide some protection against the cold and still allow the manual dexterity you need for fussy jobs.

wool, which will repel water. Down mittens are very effective until they get wet, but a vapor barrier made of plastic bags both inside and outside of down mittens can solve that problem. Plastic kitchen or surgical gloves for inside layers and large industrial rubber gloves for an outer layer will work to sandwich wool gloves. Polyester mittens don't have to be protected as carefully as down because polyester will absorb almost no water.

3M's Thinsulate is used effectively in mittens and gloves these days. And pile liners made of polyester help beat the moisture problem when worn with a breathable waterproof shell.

Losing mittens can be just as dangerous as losing a hat if you don't have a backup pair; spares are always in my pack. If the temperatures get really cold, don't feel childish about pinning your mittens to your sleeves and around your neck. Better to evoke a few laughs than to have frostbitten fingers with the dexterity of stones.

Socks

It's important here to remember that dead air spaces are the key to insulation. If you are wearing your regular hiking boots in the cold and if they were originally bought to fit over one pair of socks, don't try to cram two pairs into that space. Doing so will only squash the dead air spaces and restrict the flow of blood. So you'd be wise to buy any pair of boots large enough to be worn over *two* pairs of socks. Two pairs will give you more insulation than one pair against both summer heat and winter cold.

Again, wool is the traditional thing. Not only does it provide those dead air spaces even when wet but it also springs back into shape repeatedly after being compressed underfoot. (Nevertheless, you'll still want to carry an extra pair or two.) Wool, in addition, draws moisture away from your feet where it could conduct heat from your skin.

But "technical fabrics" have gotten into the act in socks, too. Various versions of polyester and polypropylene are used in combination with wool or by themselves to produce socks that wick moisture away from your skin quickly and dry out in a wind, or a nod, or at least by morning. Hydrofil and Thermax are two of the names you'll see attached to socks.

Speaking of moisture, the vapor-barrier system works on your feet as well as on the rest of your body. This system can be particularly helpful when there is a chance of leaky boots. Black Diamond sells a vapor barrier sock for the purpose, or you can use the versatile plastic bag. The best layering method if you're *not* wearing waterproof boots is to start with thin wool socks followed by a vapor barrier. Plastic next to the skin feels uncomfortable and may cause blisters. Over the first vapor barrier, put heavy wool socks and then another vapor barrier. Your feet will sweat with this arrangement since there's no way to ventilate them, yet they will stay warm.

Insoles

As resilient as wool socks are, they tend to stay in a permanent state of compression when you are just standing around. These periods of inactivity are also when you are most likely to become chilled and when the warmth-giving flow of blood to your feet is likely to be reduced. To combat the situation, the use of insoles in your footwear is recommended. Felt insoles are the best because they provide insulation while compressing very little. Real lambskin comes in a close second. Both materials, like wool socks, transfer moisture away from your feet. In order to get a proper fit, it's wise to buy insoles at the same time you're buying your boots.

Trail Footwear

Boots for skiing and snowshoeing are covered in Chapter 11. For biking, canoeing, and hiking several possibilities are available. When it's cold enough to get out of regular cycling shoes, it's probably too cold to bike. But you can bolster the insulation around your feet by using a vapor barrier inside your shoe and by wearing a pair of heavy wool socks *over* your shoes. Gaiters that come down well over the tops of your feet will also help. Performance has a new Neoprene Shoe Cover that has long been needed for cold weather cycling.

Canoeists who aren't planning to do much walking won't need a lot of ankle and arch support. So they can get away with felt liners inside a pair of buckle galoshes. The galoshes will keep weight to a minimum while providing a waterproof outer shell for those soggy launchings and landings.

Hikers have many options in footwear for cold weather. I've used regular hiking boots in the snow. Yet even well-treated leather will eventually get wet, causing freeze-up problems, particularly at night. You'll find that a multilayered midsole, plenty of water-repellent, and the use of gaiters will all help reduce heat loss in leather boots.

Rubber is another possibility. It keeps the wet out, but it also keeps the sweat in. You can keep your socks dry with a vapor barrier, or you can change socks frequently. In either case, I'd use a double-layer, all-rubber boot that has insulation sandwiched between the layers.

Because I object to wet feet, I've finally settled on using the boot that made Bean famous—L.L. Bean's Maine Hunting Shoe, that is. These have rubber bottoms and leather tops. The style I prefer has felt liners and tops about 9 inches high. The rubber keeps the water out of the most vulnerable part of the boot; the leather lets a good deal of the sweat escape (if you don't use a vapor barrier), and the removable liners have always succeeded in keeping my feet warm in temperatures that drop well below 0° F. I'd recommend taking at least one pair of extra felt liners on anything longer than a day trip. Also, if you waterproof the leather and wear breathable

Northern Outfitters

Boots with foam insulation may be needed to keep your feet warm at extremely low temperatures.

gaiters, it's almost impossible for moisture to get in but still possible for it to get out.

L.L. Bean isn't the only company to make boots of this sort. Sorel, a Canadian company, makes similar boots that Linda has used for several years with great satisfaction. However, beware of cheap imitations that have shoddy workmanship and inferior rubber and leather.

For truly arctic conditions—temperatures consistently well below 0° F.—I'm told that those strange looking rubber boots, called Mickey Mouse boots and made for the U.S. Army, are great. They consist of two layers of rubber with air sealed between them (dead air space). What bothers me about them is that if the air goes, there goes the insulation. Twenty miles from nowhere, I'd rather not have a sharp stick poke a hole in my warmth.

When expecting really extreme conditions, I'd spring for a boot made by Northern Outfitters of Utah. At the heart of their Expedition Series Boots is polyurethane foam that will keep your toes toasty at 30 below and below.

Gaiters

Gaiters that are not breathable cause a lot of condensation. So Gore-Tex is a good choice. For years, I've used gaiters made of canvas for all but the warmest and slushiest of cold weather. Outdoor Research has come up with the Crocodile Gaiters which adjust to fit any boot you might wear. They have a hook and loop closure system that gives you full-length adjustability. Their lower section is coated waterproof nylon while their uppers are Gore-Tex/Taslan.

In-Camp Footwear

Having warm and comfortable footwear to put on after you've set up camp is rather like having bedroom slippers to put on when you get home. Besides, the use of some kind of booties, as they're called, will help keep snow and moisture out of your tent.

Down and polyester are the usual insulations used, and as usual I'd suggest polyester. Look for booties that have elastic across the instep to hold them in place and a drawstring in the top to keep them up. An Ensolite insole is common, but the thing to look at carefully is the outer sole. Leather and rip-stop nylon are treacherously slippery when used as outer soles. Instead, make sure you get Cordura nylon soles. They aren't exactly slipproof, but they're much better than the others.

Clothing Sizes and the Layer Principle

As effective as the layer principle is in theory, it remains so in practice only when you wear clothing of the right sizes. That objective is not always as simple as it sounds. Consider the problem.

Let's say you usually wear a medium-size shirt and jacket. So you start to dress by putting on a net shirt, a turtleneck, and a wool shirt. These feel fairly comfortable. But when you add a sweater, things begin to feel a bit tight.

On top of these layers you add a medium-size polyester jacket, and you definitely feel the pinch. Finally comes the medium-size parka shell. Now you feel and look like an overstuffed scarecrow. Besides that, the dead air spaces in your clothing have been considerably compressed, greatly decreasing their insulative value. In addition, the tight-fitting clothes can restrict your blood circulation.

The obvious point so often overlooked is that you grow in bulk with each layer of clothes you put on. By the time you get out to the last few layers, you're ready for a larger size. Some manufacturers, being well aware of this problem, will purposely oversize their outer garments. When you buy outer clothing, try it on over everything else you think you might wear on a winter trip. Only then can you be sure of a comfortable fit and a layer system that will perform at top efficiency.

The layer system of insulation depends on outer garments that are large enough to fit comfortably over the inner layers.

10

Snow Camp

I have never considered myself crazy. But two years ago when I returned from a weekend camping trip, a middle-aged fellow I'd never seen before said I was nuts.

The two days of camping had been just what my friend George and I had needed to clear our heads. We'd used cross-country skis to get back into the high country where the ice fishing had been really hot and where deer and elk had provided the opportunity for some exciting wildlife photography. The days had been clear and the nights cold. We'd had superb meals of fresh fish. In the evenings we'd been pleasantly pooped and had slept soundly in the snugness of our sleeping bags. All things considered, it had been a very comfortable and refreshing trip.

Back at the parking lot as we unshouldered our packs, I noticed that we were being watched by a man who'd brought his kids to go sledding on a nearby hill. Within ten minutes his curiosity had gotten the better of him, and he ambled over.

"Afternoon. You guys have a cabin back in there?"

"Nope," George said, "that's all National Forest land; I don't think there's a cabin within twenty miles."

"Well, what ya doin' with all that gear?"

I was a little puzzled at this point but explained that we'd been camping for two nights. The man was amazed.

"You mean you've been living outside in the snow! Do you know it got down to 5 below last night? You guys gotta be nuts."

At the time I can remember being amused at the man's reaction. I have discovered, however, that an awful lot of people cringe at the thought of camping in cold weather. Many of these people are ardent campers during the warm months. But for some reason, they think they have to stop going on overnight outings once there's frost or snow on the ground.

The fact is that cold-weather camping can be quite comfortable and safe if you put some thought into your clothing (Chapter 9), your shelter, your sleeping gear, and your winter kitchen.

Shelter

Tent

The use of a tent for your winter shelter is probably the easiest way to start. You may even be able to use a tent you already have. Just be sure that the tent has a pole arrangement that won't sink into the snow. Any of the free-standing models, whether dome, wedge, tunnel,

A two-man tent can be made suitable for winter camping with the addition of a vestibule that can be used for storing bulky gear.

or some other exotic design, will work. Even the traditional mountain tent is suitable if it has an A-frame pole arrangement in which the pole bottoms are anchored into tabs or grommets at the tent corners. The only other musts for a winter tent are that it be breathable and that it have a waterproof floor. A single-layer tent that doesn't breathe will trap water from condensation on the inside, turning your shelter into an ice-encrusted cave.

Recent technology has made it possible to manufacture waterproof and breathable single-walled tents. Once the outside temperature drops much below freezing, water vapor will condense and freeze on the inside of these tents. As the moisture freezes, it locks into the fibers of the material, so very little of it will fall on you. But it is difficult to get the frozen moisture out of the material until it melts.

There are a few other features that might make a tent more livable for you in the snow.

• *Size*—I've spent many a winter-camping trip in a two-man tent, but I must admit that larger (and heavier) tents are more comfortable for two people and their gear. Perhaps the middle ground between the lighter weight and the added room is a two-man tent with a vestibule. Vestibules are usually floorless, yet they are ideal for storing gear or for cooking, if you absolutely must cook inside.

• *Cook Holes*—Again, when cooking in the tent becomes a necessity, it's much better to have the stove sitting on the snow than to have it sitting on the tent floor. A cook hole, which is a zippered hole in the floor, will allow you to do this. This feature decreases the likelihood that a knocked-over stove will start a fire, and it helps delineate the kitchen area, the zone where arms and elbows should be wary of flames and hot pots.

• *Frost Liners*—A frost liner is usually a layer of cotton fabric that is hung inside from the ceiling of an A-frame tent, close to, but not touching, the roof. The idea is that this additional ceiling will allow moist air to pass through it without condensing since the liner will raise the inside air temperature above the dew point. The moist air is then carried directly out the vent, leaving no dampness inside.

In fact, some moisture always does get in the frost liner. But cotton, unlike nylon, traps the ice crystals in its fibers instead of letting them snow down on you and your gear. That's the theory.

My experience with frost liners has been that they reduce the living space in a tent just enough to make brushing the liner with your back and arms inevitable. So ice crystals do drop on you. In short, I can't see that frost liners are worth the effort to carry and hang, although some experienced winter campers to find them helpful.

• *Snow Flaps*—Flaps of material sewn along the bottom of the tent on the outside are supposed to be covered with snow to help keep the tent anchored and to help keep wind from blowing underneath it. They are hardly worth having unless you plan on a lot of winter camping above timberline.

Pitching a Tent in the Snow

In the summer, pitching a tent isn't much of a hassle, but when you contend with frozen ground or snow, things are different. On frozen ground, tent pegs must be replaced by stumps, trees, bushes, logs, or

Recreational Equipment, Inc.
A roomy, free-standing tent is a good choice for snow camping.

rocks. This is a time when free-standing tents really come into their own.

When the ground is covered with snow, you're faced with other problems. The tricky thing is pitching the tent so it remains taut against the wind or the weight of accumulating snow. Your first concern will be to pack down a tent base. Skis or snowshoes serve admirably for the purpose. You'll find that it helps to keep your pack on since the added weight makes for a firmer base. By stomping and jumping on the snow, you can make both a level and a firm tent site. Tent pegs will hold fairly well, and you won't sink out of sight in soft fluff when you climb inside for the night. I once watched a novice winter camper collapse his tent about his ears because he hadn't prepared a proper base.

A good packing job will also allow you to walk around the tent site without skis or snowshoes—a luxury you'll greatly appreciate, particularly when nature calls in the middle of the night.

When the base is ready, you have several choices for securing the tent. Skis, ski poles, and snowshoes are all excellent for winter tent pegs because they can be sunk deep in the snow. If you use them, however, you'll have to stay close to camp or drop your tent before venturing out. Sometimes dead tree limbs can be found to act as pegs, but I'd generally plan on bringing special snow pegs. Wide, cuped, or angular pegs made of plastic or aluminum and measuring 8 to 12 inches long are effective. When you put these pegs into the snow, it's a good idea to stomp them down firmly with the heel of your boot. I sometimes even pour a little water around each peg. Once it freezes, things really stay in place.

For an alternative to tent pegs you can improvise your own "deadmen." How's that for an ominous sounding device? Actually a deadman is simply a guyline anchor that is buried in the snow. Both skis and snowshoes can be used in this way, each one acting as an anchor for several tent lines. There are also special deadmen, called snow flukes, which you can buy. Flukes are broad-faced aluminum affairs about the size and shape of the blade of a dirt shovel. A fairly long nylon loop is attached to the center of each fluke so a guyline can be tied to it after the fluke is buried. Because these devices tend to dig in deeper when pulled on, they're effective under windy conditions.

Snow Cave

One of the warmest and most comfortable shelters can be made from the snow itself in the form of a snow cave. Snow is an extremely effective insulator, when you aren't in direct contact with it, and it protects you from the wind when you are surrounded by it.

There's no big secret to constructing a comfortable snow cave, but you should know some basic pointers. To start with you'll need a couple of lightweight shovels; aluminum-bladed shovels with detachable wooden handles are handy. You'll also need to spend an hour or two of wet, physical work. So wear waterproof outer garments, and start your work well before dark. A good snow cave requires compacted snow about six feet deep. Drifts on the lee side of ridges usually offer ideal conditions. However, take extreme caution in steep mountainous areas where excellent snow-cave conditions may coincide with excellent avalanche conditions (see Chapter 12).

Start your snow cave by digging a 3' x 3' entrance tunnel into the face of the snow drift. The ceiling of the tunnel should be arched to provide structural support, and should extend into the snow for three or four feet. Because of the cramped quarters, this is a one-man job. Trade off on the digging. While one person works on the tunnel, another person can push the excavated snow downslope to form a flat entrance platform.

Several variations are possible in the snow-cave proper. It can consist of one dome-shaped room—a 7' x 7' room high enough to sit up in is quite adequate to house four people and their gear. Or it can have one to three sleeping alcoves 4' wide, 4' high and 7' long. These alcoves, which radiate off the entrance tunnel will each sleep two people, and you'll have a community cooking area where the alcoves meet the entrance.

In either case, dig the living area slightly higher than the entrance tunnel to help keep cold air out. Also arch the ceiling to form a good structural support, and smooth off rough edges that would form natural drip spots once the cave is warmed by body heat and the operations of the cook stove. As you dig out the cave, one person should remain near the entrance to throw loose snow outside while the other person does the heavy work.

Once the cave is dug out to your satisfaction, there are two important things to do before moving in:

• First, with the basket of your ski pole poke a vent hole through the ceiling to the outside. This will allow proper ventilation while you're cooking.

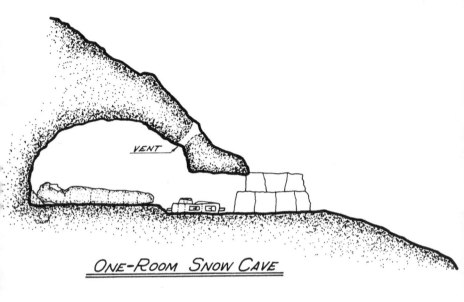

ONE-ROOM SNOW CAVE

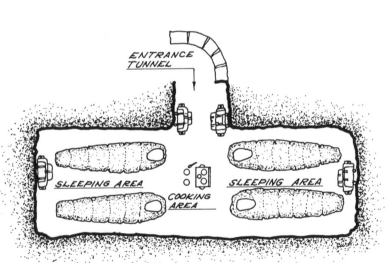

ALCOVE SNOW CAVE

Snow is extremely effective insulation, and a shelter made out of it can be snug and warm despite frigid temperatures outside. Size can be varied to suit the number of campers.

• Second, using solid chunks of snow remaining from your digging process, construct a windbreak around the entrance to help prevent snow from drifting it closed. Keep your shovels inside, by the way, in case you do have to dig yourself out after a night storm. I've been in a snow cave where the vent and entrance were covered by two feet of new snow during the night. When I awoke to my own labored breathing, you can bet it was reassuring to have a shovel close at hand!

Although thoughts of cave-ins and suffocation haunt some snow-cave dwellers, a properly constructed snow cave is very stable. And if the vent hole and entrance do get snowed over, your own difficulty in breathing will make you aware of the fact. The breathing difficulty will even wake you out of a sound sleep, and you can then clear away the snow.

Sleeping Gear

A good sleeping bag and pad are two essential items in a winter camp.

Sleeping Bag

While discussing the pros and cons of down and polyester as sleeping-bag fillers for use in wet weather, I came out firmly on the side of polyester. When it comes to winter camping, I can't be so positive. Down can be used in cold weather when used with a vapor barrier. If the sleeping bag shell is water-repellent, little moisture will enter from the outside, provided the temperature remains cold. A vapor-barrier liner will keep moisture from entering from the inside and will prevent evaporative heat loss. The price of a good down bag, however, is not cheap. So polyester bags are still very much in the winter running.

• *Down-bag Construction*—The price of down is not the only factor contributing to the high cost of sleeping bags made with this filler. The nature of down itself requires some construction practices that are more costly than those used in many polyester bags. Down is shifty. If it isn't contained in relatively small compartments, it flows to the bottom of the sleeping-bag shell. So in the construction of a down bag, the fill must be evenly distributed in a series of horizontal tubes, usually about 6 inches wide, made by sewing baffles between inner and outer shells.

So-called box construction is the easiest method and the least expensive to make. The technique is to sew the top and bottom of each baffle directly above and below one another as the baffle is attached to the outer and inner shell. Unfortunately, this practice makes for cold spots in the bag because there are places at each baffle where the down cannot flow to provide insulation.

Slant-box construction solves this problem by attaching the baffles at an angle so no connecting seams are directly above or below one another. Down then flows into the corners of the tubes, which overlap each other, providing for continuous insulation. This method of construction is the most widely used for down bags.

Less popular, but even more efficient, is what's called overlap or "V" construction, so named because the interior baffles resemble a line of V's with their tops touching one another. This is the best design for restricting down shift. (Some people believe it also restricts the loft.) But "V" construction requires more material and more work to produce. It's found in only the most expensive bags.

• *Polyester-bag Construction*—Whether continuous or staple fibers (see page 134) are used, a great deal of the efficiency of a bag depends on how the polyester batts are attached to the shell of the sleeping bag. Sewn-through construction is the cheapest and least effective. The stitches go directly through the batt and the shell of the sleeping bag in a quilted fashion that causes cold spots. This quilting method can be used effectively only if two or three layers of batting are sandwiched together so that the sewn-through seams don't fall opposite one another. This sandwiched method of construction is commonly called offset quilting and is used extensively in polyester bags that have insulation of staple fibers.

In a method called edge-stabilized construction, the batt is sewn to the shell only around the edges. This type of construction is used with the continuous-fiber batts because they hold together something like a pad of steel wool. Two or three layers of edge-stabilized batts are often sandwiched together to achieve the desired loft in a bag.

Finally, there's the batt-baffle system. Polyester batts are sewn to the shell in a way that resembles a series of slant-tube baffles in a down bag. Each batt-baffle overlaps the next by half its width forming a double thickness of insulation at all places.

• *Common features*—After all the differences between polyester and down bags have been examined, you're still left with some considerations that are common to both types.

The question of zipper length remains the same whether you're considering a down or a polyester bag. A zipper is a logical place for drafts to develop, so the shorter it is, the more efficient the bag will be. Make sure that any zipper has a good draft baffle covering its entire length.

The shape of your bag is another common concern. You'll find mummy and semimummy bags the best for winter use. They will conform most closely to your body contours and, therefore, will be warmer, lighter, and less bulky than a rectangular or semirectangular bag. In addition, a mummy bag can be closed around your head so that just your nose sticks out. You'll want that feature when the temperature plunges.

After such things as construction, design, zippers, and shape have been taken into consideration, loft is the standard indicator of sleeping-bag warmth. The thicker the bag, the warmer it will keep you. But there are some subtleties to the matter. Most manufacturers' loft figures indicate the total thickness of their bags (both layers). However, it's the amount of insulation *over* you that does most of the insulating. So some manufacturers put more filler in the top layer of their bags than in the bottom layer, relying on the sleeping pad to do most of the insulating beneath the user.

As a rough guide for top-quality bags, I'd suggest the following figures for loft/comfort-range ratios:

Total Loft	*Minimum Comfort Range (° F.)*
2″	50
4″	40
6″	20
7″	0
7″ (5″ over you)	−10
8″ (5″ over you)	−20

To increase loft, don't overlook the possibility of using a sleeping-bag liner or cover to turn a three-season bag into something suitable for winter.

Sleeping Pads

The only sensible choice for a winter mattress is a closed-cell pad. Open-cell pads are much too likely to absorb water. Air mattresses take on the temperature of the surrounding air, making them useless when it's cold. For a more complete discussion of mattresses and pads see Chapter 3.

Shelter and Sleeping Gear in Action

It may seem simplistic to talk about how to live in a tent or a snow cave, but subtleties do exist. First, remember that darkness descends early on winter days. A tent camp may take 45 minutes to set up exactly as you'd like it; a snow cave may take twice as long or longer. So find a protected campsite well before dark and get things established.

The nuances of living in a tent start at the door. Before putting any packs or other equipment inside, make sure snow and ice that may be clinging to things has been knocked off. A hand-sized whisk broom is very handy for this task; it also serves as an excellent tool to brush snow off your clothes and boots. If you don't go through this snow-removal process before climbing into your tent, the snow that comes in with you invariably ends up under your sleeping bag or inside your clothes. Snow-covered boots are the worst offenders, so I make a point of sitting in the tent door with my feet outside and changing into my insulated booties before climbing in.

To help keep snow out of your tent, take your boots off at the door and put on down or polyester booties.

Once you're inside the tent or snow cave, the first order of business is to spread out your sleeping pad for insulation. Before taking out your sleeping bag you may want to test your unmade bed for lumps. The snow camper has an advantage when it comes to fashioning a comfortable sleeping place. Snow can be contoured to fit your favorite sleeping position. If there isn't a suitable indentation for your hip or shoulder, just pound one out. With a little practice and patience, you can custom make a contoured bed to fit every bulge and bend of your anatomy.

A closed-cell sleeping pad isn't the softest mattress in the world, so you can use extra clothes between your pad and your sleeping bag to pad those body spots that like to be pampered. The clothes will add extra insulation too.

Since your kidney area seems to be especially vulnerable to the cold while you're sleeping, a sweater laid out flat under the small of your back can be a big help. An empty pack put under your feet will keep them off the cold tent floor if you don't have a full-length pad.

Despite all the insulation you may stuff underneath you, there may be times when you awake in the middle of the night with a chill. There are several things you can do. First, check to make sure your head and shoulders haven't come uncovered, and be sure your wool hat is still on. Yes, it's good form and good sense to wear a hat to bed when you're winter camping. If you're still cold after battening down all hatches, try flexing arm and leg muscles for several minutes. This can be a surprisingly effective way to shake a chill. A few shots of high-energy food like candy and nuts will boost your heat output too.

Getting out of bed in the morning requires fortitude. You roll over and notice the sides of your tent have brightened. Companions start to stir in their sleeping bags. "Five more minutes," you say to yourself and snuggle deeper into the warm sleeping bag. Someone speaks. Maybe a low curse, confirming your sense of the temperature outside. Reluctantly, you resign yourself to the process of emerging from your bag—usually with the movements and appearance of some ancient bird hatching from its shell.

Here again the process can be made easier by practicing some subtleties. First, don't get out of the bag until you have opened the tent door, leaned out, and started the coffee water warming on the stove. Next, push your sleeping bag to your waist and put on shirt, sweater, parka—whatever you need to face the morning temperature. Now, quickly extract your legs and pull on the pants that have been kept warm beneath you all night. Pull on down booties, grab your boots, and climb out to a hot cup of coffee.

Unless you follow the practice of some callous souls who take their

If you hang your cross-country ski boots around your neck, they will warm next to your body while you have breakfast and will be comfortable to wear by the time you're ready to break camp or head out on skis.

boots to bed with them, your boots will be frigid. The best solution I've found for that problem is to tie both laces together and drape the boots around my neck so they'll hang inside my parka under my arms. When I've had my fill of hot oatmeal and coffee, the boots are warm, and I'm ready to head off for a morning of cross-country skiing.

The Kitchen

A snow cave at 10,000 feet in the mountains of Montana may seem like a strange place for a kitchen, much less a fondly remembered kitchen. Yet such a spot holds a special place in my culinary memory bank as a "cold kitchen" that provided copious amounts of warmth, companionship, and good food. I've known other memorable winter kitchens, such as the one that served up Savory Stew amidst elk and bison in the Lamar Valley. And I'll never forget John's kitchen that capped an extraordinary chicken curry with dessert of cheese cake and Irish coffee—all at a temperature reading of −5° F.

As different as these kitchens and their menus were, however, they had two common denominators. Each one was safe, and each one was efficient. When you're cooking and living in snow, cold, and wind, these are special considerations. You've got to pay close attention to your stove and its use, to getting and storing water, and to a number of other kitchen matters.

Stove Selection

In most camps, a stove should be the center of a winter kitchen. Firewood is usually frozen beneath the snow. Besides, cooking over a fire is much less efficient than cooking over a stove. Even if you can find plenty of downed, dead wood where the use of a warming and cooking fire won't degrade the environment, be sure to scatter the dead coals and ashes upon breaking camp. Otherwise, the melting snow of spring will leave ugly fire rings perched in the most peculiar places. Never depend entirely on a fire either; a stove should go along on any winter trip for use in an emergency.

Despite the wide variety of backpacking stoves, few of them are satisfactory for the winter backpacker, skier, or snowshoer. First to fall by the trailside are alcohol and butane stoves.

Although alcohol stoves have the advantage of being extremely light, and although they require no priming, their heat output is too low for the demands of winter use, which often include melting snow for water.

Butane becomes inefficient at low temperatures. It won't vaporize below 32° F. at sea level. And even though lower atmospheric pressure allows it to function down to 13° F. at 10,000 feet, it's hardly the kind of fuel you'd want to bet your winter dinners on.

Kerosene stoves offer the heat output needed in a cold-weather kitchen. And they don't require insulation from the snow as do some white-gas stoves. They do, though, need a separate priming fuel to get them started. Although the amount of this priming fuel—usually white gas—is tiny, it means carrying an additional container and going through another step to get the stove going.

Self-pressurized white-gas stoves also require priming, but that can be done with the white gas itself. In cold weather, they must be insulated from the snow in order to maintain enough tank pressure for proper operation. Cold-weather use of these self-pressurized stoves has become somewhat more efficient with the use of an accessory pump that can be bought separately. It makes starting these stoves a bit easier.

In the long run, however, the heavier white gas stoves with built-in pressure pumps are the best bet for heat output of the blowtorch variety. They have fuel capacities of 10 to 16 ounces, and most will operate on simmer for at least 2 hours. These features mean fast and simple starts, a hot flame, and a burning time that's long enough to cook a complete meal in winter, even if you must melt snow for water. The major drawback of white gas is that it's very flammable. It needs special attention to be used safely, particularly in a winter kitchen, where a burned hand or tent involves a far greater risk than it might in milder weather.

Stove Location

Where you use your stove is a major safety consideration. Outside in the open air is the best place for a winter kitchen. You have plenty of room to maneuver. There's no problem with ventilation, and a knocked-over stove will not set the snow afire. If you're really cold, you can get into your sleeping bag inside your tent and still operate a stove that's outside on the snow. The big drawback with this outside set-up is the wind. A stove that's exposed to windy conditions may take twice as long to cook your meal. To protect a stove, packs can be used as shields, aluminum foil will serve as a wind screen, or you can dig a stove alcove right into the snow.

When the wind really starts to howl, however, you'll be forced to move into a snow cave or a tent to protect both yourself and the stove. A cave is a safer place to cook than a tent because you are still surrounded by snow. The fire hazard isn't great if you keep clothing and sleeping bags out of the kitchen. Ventilation is a concern. Have a vent hole poked through the roof of the cave near the stove, and don't block the cave entrance. Stoves eat up a surprising amount of oxygen, and carbon-monoxide poisoning is a real danger. If snow is falling, check vents and the entrance frequently while cooking to make sure they don't drift over.

Cooking in a tent is quite hazardous. On top of the concern with ventilation, you have the fire danger. In confined quarters where you're wearing bulky clothing, you're unlikely to be the epitome of grace in motion. A gloved hand or a bundled elbow can knock the cook stove onto your sleeping bag or against the tent. And despite the words of Sam McGee, the interior of a fiery furnace is not what he makes it out to be.

A tent kitchen requires constant attention. If at all possible, fuel and light the stove outside; get it running smoothly before bringing it inside. Use the cook hole if your tent floor has one. Keep the kitchen neatly organized. Keep tent vents open. And have an emergency plan in mind should the stove get knocked over. The importance of caution can't be stressed enough.

Stove Use

Whether you're in a tent, in a snow cave, or outside, there are some special considerations that go into using a stove in your winter kitchen. Before you ever start on a trip, make sure you'll be carrying fresh fuel. Coleman Fuel is probably the most readily available source of white gas. It has an effective shelf-life of about three years, if the can is unopened. An open can of white gas starts to lose full potency after about six months.

In planning the amount of fuel to carry, you can figure about a quarter of a pint for the average 4-man meal cooked under calm conditions. You'll have to double that figure if you'll cook in the wind. If melting snow is your only source of water, you'll also have to double that quarter-pint figure.

Before you put your stove in your pack, make sure it is clean and in good operating order. Don't assume it will work; start it up, using some of the fuel you plan to take on the trip.

Filling a stove before every meal is especially important in the winter when cooking takes more time and when running out of fuel in the middle of preparing the main course is more than an inconvenience. When using a self-pressurized stove, remember to fill it no more than 80 percent of capacity so there's enough room left in the tank to build the vapor pressure needed for efficient operation.

A fuel can with a built-in pour spout helps in the efficiency of the filling operation. When using cans without spouts, bring a funnel so you're sure not to waste any fuel. In either case, taking off and putting on fuel caps requires some manual dexterity that can't be achieved while you're wearing mittens and may even be difficult with gloves on. This is where your silk glove liners come in handy. Speaking of fuel caps, if possible attach the cap to the neck of the fuel bottle with a string. A fuel cap is small enough to get quickly buried in the snow, and a capless bottle is useless on the trail.

Stoves that must be primed before use (and even some pump stoves require this operation when the temperature drops below freezing), can be primed with the kind of fire-starting paste that comes in a squeeze tube. This tactic eliminates the possibility of spillage and waste that is inherent in a liquid primer. You may find that your stove must be primed several times in cold weather before it's hot enough to build its own operating pressure. Dont' attempt to reprime or refuel a stove that is still hot, however. I've seen several people burned by fuel that was ignited in this way.

Once the stove is going and burning evenly, regulate the flame to conserve fuel. Don't let the thing roar full blast when nothing's on the burner. Also, keep the flame burning *under* the pot, not licking around its sides where the heat does no good.

Finally, even in winter winds, don't shield a stove too closely or it may overheat, blowing out the safety valve and shooting a stream of flame across your kitchen.

Getting and Storing Water

Water is an elusive commodity in the winter. You can be surrounded by it in its frozen and crystalline form. But unless you camp by an open stream or lake, you're without a convenient supply. Sucking snow while on the trail may be somewhat refreshing. It will hardly quench a real thirst, though, and it can chill your stomach to the point where you'll get a bellyache along with the shivers.

Often the only way to get water in enough quantity to do any good is to melt snow or ice. Quantity is important. Not only is water needed to cook the freeze-dried food that usually constitutes the bulk of winter backpacking meals, but drinking water—and lots of it—is needed to keep you from getting dehydrated.

Dry winter air, particularly at high altitudes, can whisk moisture from your skin so quickly that you're often unaware of sweating. Nevertheless, your body loses a great deal of water during the exertion of a ski or snowshoe trip. That water must be replaced or you'll lose much of your resistance to fatigue, frostbite, and hypothermia.

When at all possible, get water from an open source. Lakes and streams often remain unfrozen even when the temperature drops well below zero. Getting to the source is sometimes a problem if high snow banks have built up along its edge. It's wise to carry a wide-mouth plastic water bottle with about 12 feet of cord tied to the neck. While you hang onto the end of the cord, you can throw the bottle into the water and retrieve it while you remain on skis or showshoes at a safe distance from the edge of the bank.

This method of getting water can be used in camp to fill all available water containers, or it can be used on the trail just to fill canteens. To stretch the water in a canteen while traveling on a waterless trail, add snow to a partially empty bottle. The snow will soon turn to water from the agitation caused by your movement.

Although melting snow on your stove takes a lot of time and fuel, it's a standard operation in a winter kitchen. Because powder snow gives the lowest water yield, try to dig beneath new snow layers to find older more coarsely crystalized snow. It will have a greater water content. If you have a little water left in your canteen, pour it into the

A wide-mouthed water bottle with 12 or 15 feet of cord tied to the neck will allow you to retrieve water without getting too close to the edges of unstable snowbanks along streams.

pot before you add snow. This step will speed up the melting process and prevent the pot from scorching and giving the water an unpleasant taste. When no water is available, add just a small amount of snow and let that melt before adding more.

Storing water overnight so you have a good supply for an easy breakfast is a problem. Water left in pots or water bottles may freeze solid. Although aluminum bottles can be heated over a stove, the process hardly makes for a quick morning start. I've discovered that a wineskin filled with hot water just before going to bed makes a wonderfully warm hot-water bottle and provides instant water for morning coffee, juice, or whatever. Leakage is no problem if you tighten the cap. I carry a 1½-liter wineskin with a small plastic funnel for no-spill filling. Some backpackers take their plastic or aluminum water bottles to bed, but to me that seems like snuggling up to an armadillo instead of a Teddy Bear.

Carrying water on the trail is a much easier task. Your movement will usually keep even cold water from freezing. And hot, sugared tea put in a canteen in the morning will stay warm for hours if it's wrapped in a sleeping bag or in spare clothing.

Food and the Kitchen in Action

The biggest element in making for a smooth-running winter kitchen is the kind of food you buy before the trip ever gets started. The cold-weather cook will sing praises to simple meals and curse the seven-course spread. On the other hand, you want to make sure you get plenty of calories. While you might get fat sitting at home eating 2,500 calories, you'll need about 4,000 calories daily to keep your heat and energy machinery running while you're on a ski or snowshoe trip. Lots of cocoa and hot cereal with sugar is fine for breakfast. Cheese, sausage, nuts, and candy can be nibbled all day for lunch. Soup and an imaginative potpourri serve as dinner. Add butter or margarine to the soup to increase your fat intake. Potatoes, pasta, or rice provides a base of carbohydrates for any potpourri, and dump in cheese, fish, or

Keys to a smooth-working winter kitchen are to have everything within easy reach and to have your stove protected from the wind.

meat for protein. You can get a precooked, three-ounce meat bar from many of the backpacking supply catalogues that is equal to a pound of raw meat and contains 550 calories. It's ideal for an addition to your dinner pot.

Two pots are all you need to prepare these hot meals. One pot is the "water pot" and is used for boiling water for drinks, instant soup, and other foods that can be mixed in your cup. The other pot is the "grease pot." This makes the big batch of porridge in the morning and the goulash or stew at night.

Keeping foods hot until you have a chance to eat them requires some attention. First, you should always use lids on your pots. They not only make things cook faster but they also keep them warm longer. Two pots that will stack one on top of the other are extremely useful for keeping two dishes warm over a one-burner stove. The main dish that has to cook goes on the bottom; the hot water "dish" that just needs to be kept warm goes on top with a lid covering it. When you do have to take a pot off the stove, setting it on a foam pad instead of the snow has obvious advantages.

After a meal, the winter wash-up chore is simple. Any dirty dishes and pots should be scraped out with a spoon and rubbed out with snow. If each member of the group always uses his own eating utensils, there isn't much chance of germs doing damage in cold weather. What little bit of stew may be left on the greasepot tonight will add seasoning to tomorrow's oatmeal. Your bowels will take to that arrangement much more readily than to soapy residue left because of insufficient rinse water.

A final consideration in the winter kitchen is the garbage detail. Pieces of foil and plastic bags tend to get overlooked and covered up very easily in the snow. So take special care in checking the kitchen floor after each meal. Small wire sealers for plastic bags are especially prone to disappear. To avoid this problem, use plastic bags that are large enough to close by tying a knot in the bag's neck. Obviously, any garbage you produce should be packed out.

11

On the Snowy Trail

Undoubtedly, winter is the trickiest time for dealing with transportation problems. When snow isn't too deep, you can continue to hike. Cold weather doesn't have to deter the cyclist either, provided he's prepared for the wind chill. But roadways covered with ice or snow don't make for very enjoyable biking. For the canoeist, the biggest danger is an unplanned plunge into icy water. Really serious cold-weather canoeists should go prepared with a full wet suit including mittens, booties, and hood. And they should paddle only where immediate rescue and permanent shelter are available.

Yet when all is said and done, the winter camper usually has to look to a different kind of transportation when the ground is buried beneath the snow. He must look to those old standbys—skis and snowshoes.

It may be reassuring to know that people have been tromping around in the snow for a long time. The earliest evidence of "foot extenders" worn to facilitate snow travel dates from 4,000 B.C. in Central Asia. These contraptions enabled our ancestors to migrate north into what we now know as the Nordic countries and Russia and into North America via the Bering Land Bridge.

Snowshoes became the favored means of winter travel in North

170

America, and the Indians refined dozens of designs to fit specific needs and snow conditions. When the French arrived in Canada, they quickly sensed the natives' ingenuity and strapped on the big shoes too. During the French and English struggle for control of North America, snowshoes were essential items of military equipment.

Recreational snowshoeing apparently originated with the French-Canadian snowshoe clubs of the 1700s. But New England also has a long tradition of snowshoeing for pleasure. To stave off cabin fever, villagers would go on snowshoe outings that usually ended with a simple but hearty meal at a hospitable farmer's table.

Skis were more popular than snowshoes in Asia and Europe. Carvings in Norway show that skiing in that country is at least 4,000 years old. Yet it wasn't until the 1850s that John Thomson, a Norwegian immigrant, opened American eyes to the virtues of skis. For twenty years, Thomson carried the U.S. Mail from California, across the Sierra, to Nevada, a 90-mile journey that took him three days. His skis were 10 feet long and weighed 25 pounds. In his pack, he carried 60 to 70 pounds.

After Thomson showed folks what could be done with skis, recreational ski clubs started popping up across the U.S., and the challenge to the snowshoe had begun. Today, cross-country skiers far outnumber snowshoers, but there's no doubt that both means of travel have been well tested.

For the winter backpacker, snowshoes and skis each have their own

Recreational cross-country skiing has a long history as something the entire family can enjoy. IDAHO HISTORICAL SOCIETY.

advantages. In really brushy country that has deep, soft snow, snowshoes are best, particularly when a great deal of trail-breaking is expected. Snowshoes generally mean a more plodding pace than you can attain on skis, but snowshoes are easier to handle and far more stable. Skis, though, can add a bit of zip to your pace and are ideal for fairly open terrain. Although skis add more excitement and may let you cover more ground, they take some getting used to and can be tricky to handle when you're carrying a load of camping gear on your back.

Selecting Snowshoe Gear

Snowshoes

Since design affects the way snowshoes handle in different terrains and under varying snow conditions, knowing some basics will help you select a pair that's right for your intended use. Major considerations in selecting a snowshoe are flotation, traction, tracking ability, traversing ability, and weight.

• *Flotation*—This quality is particularly important for the backpacker and depends upon the surface area of the snowshoes. For example, a 10″ × 36″ design has 360 square inches of surface, which is good for a person of up to about 175 pounds. Put a 35-pound pack on that person and he'd have to go to a 10″ × 56″ model for proper flotation.

• *Traction*—In hilly or mountainous country, having a snowshoe that will climb without slipping is especially important. The position of the toe hole affects traction. The farther forward the toe hole, the more traction you will get. Also, the toe of your boot should be able to fit through the toe hole and dig into the snow. For additional grip on hard, icy snow, you can buy traction cleats or snowshoe crampons.

• *Tracking Ability*—When a snowshoe goes where you want it to go, it is said to have good tracking ability. To do this, it should be heavier in the tail than in the toe. In other words, when you pick it up by the binding or the toe hole, the tail should drop noticeably toward the ground. This weight distribution and an upswept toe keep the shoe from digging into the snow. Tracking is further enhanced by a long, pointed heel that will drag slightly and act like a rudder to keep the snowshoe pointed in the direction of your stride.

• *Traversing Ability*—A narrow design, 10 inches or less, is the best for angling across the face of a hill where you must edge the side of the shoe into the snow.

• *Weight*—The old saying that a pound on the foot is equal to five pounds on the back applies to snowshoes. The lighter they are, the less work you'll have put in by the end of a day.

After a close look at these design features, you can see that you must make certain compromises when selecting a shoe to fit the conditions you expect. For example, a narrow model is best for traversing hilly country, but a large shoe is needed for good flotation. You can make a narrow snowshoe only so long before it's as long as a ski.

When it comes to specific designs, there are five types of snowshoes worth considering.

• *Green Mountain Bearpaw*—This is a snowshoe for mountainous, wooded terrain. It is oval-shaped and narrow, with a slight upturn to the toe. The narrowness prevents downhill tilt when you traverse moderate hillsides, and the absence of a tail makes this snowshoe maneuver easily in brush and timber.

• *Cross Country*—Except for the addition of a short tail, this design is similar to the Green Mountain. The tail makes it longer by about 10 inches, so it's not quite as maneuverable. But the heel drag that you tend to get in the Green Mountain is reduced.

• *Michigan*—A tear-shaped shoe with long, narrow tail and slight upturn to the toe. It's effective for trail and sparse-forest travel. The long tail makes it track well and keeps the tips up so they don't shovel into deep snow.

• *Alaskan*—This is a long, narrow snowshoe with a real upsweep to the toe. It's good for moving out in open country and deep snow. The large support area makes this snowshoe the best for carrying heavy loads. But the length is awkward in brush and timber.

• *Ojibwa*—The Ojibwa comes closest to the Alaskan in design; it's a little wider and has a distinctive point to the tip, which is made possible by the fact that it is the only shoe made of two pieces of wood joined at toe and tail. This is another snowshoe made for open country and deep snow.

All of these designs are made with wooden frames and rawhide webbing, and some of them are available with aluminum frames and neoprene or nylon webbing. Traditionally, straight-grained ash was used for the frames. The webbing was cowhide coated with varnish to prevent water absorption. Cowhide webbing has the disadvantage of being tasty to things, like mice and porcupines, that go chomp in the night. And if these webs aren't kept liberally coated with varnish, they'll soak up water and start to sag.

Neoprene is now replacing cowhide for webbing. That's sad news for the historic-minded, but neoprene has several advantages. It is strong and water-repellent, it doesn't decay or stretch, and it requires no maintenance. Also, little critters find it quite unpalatable.

If you like to putter and don't mind the chores of varnishing and of keeping beasts away from your snowshoes, choose cowhide; it will probably last longer than neoprene. Choose the neoprene if your only concern is utility.

The aluminum frames now on the market have the virtue of being light, and most of them are strong. But they must be coated with plastic or anodized. Otherwise snow will stick to them very easily.

All-plastic snowshoes are available, but I've found them a poor choice when I'm packing a load. The plastic isn't sturdy enough, and these shoes don't have enough carrying support to keep me and my gear on top of the fluff. They are satisfactory, though, for an emergency shoe or for one to be carried on your pack for short snow crossings.

Below are the *average* weights and capacities of the various types of snowshoes.

Snowshoes	Weight (per pair)	Capacity
Green Mountain Bearpaw	4½ lbs.	10 x 36/175 lbs.
Cross Country	4⅝ lbs.	10 x 46/200 lbs.
Michigan	5 6/8 lbs.	14 x 48/225 lbs
Alaska	5⅞ lbs.	12 x 60/225 lbs.
Ojibwa	5lbs.	12 x 60/200 lbs.
Aluminum Frame	4⅛ lbs.	9 x 30/150 lbs.
Aluminum Frame	5 lbs.	10 x 43/200 lbs.
Plastic	3½ lbs.	12 x 30/175 lbs.

Bindings

A dozen types of snowshoe bindings are available, many of them very similar. You can choose between two of them and be prepared for any kind of country.

The "H" type of binding is the lightest and least expensive; you can get it in rawhide or neoprene. I'd suggest neoprene, even if you're a purist. The neoprene doesn't stretch, so you won't have to stop and adjust your straps all the time. A good "H" binding has a piece of material that curves around the tip of your boot in addition to the piece that goes over your toe. The tip piece keeps your foot from sliding forward when you go downhill. The heel strap on this binding should be connected to the outer edge of the snowshoe to minimize sideways heel slip. This is a good binding for flat and rolling country. But when you start traversing something that resembles a real hill, your heels will slip.

When you head for the hills, go to the Sherpa binding. This binding comes with Sherpa snowshoes, but you can buy the bindings separately. Basically, these are modern modifications of the "H" binding, but the hinged toe plate is secured to the webbing to give lateral support. The binding is made of neoprene and has hooks, "D" rings, and buckled heel strap for securing your boots.

Foot Gear

Oldtime snowshoers swear by high, Indian-style moccasins worn over heavy pairs of socks. Because moccasins don't have heels and are soft, they cause very little wear on the snowshoe webbing. In addition, moccasins are light and conform comfortably to the contours of your feet. They're hard to come by, though, and they're expensive.

An inexpensive compromise is a pair of felt boot liners under buckle overshoes. The combination is warm, relatively light, and pliable. Also, the rubber is so soft that it won't cause much wear to the webbing. The trick is to get the right combination of overshoe and liner. The fit should be snug enough to prevent blistering and chafing and yet should allow adequate blood circulation and foot movement. You'll have to shop around to get the right fit.

Some snowshoers who use this overshoe-liner combination complain that even though the felt absorbs much of their foot moisture their feet still get damp and cold after a day on the trail. The rubber overshoe doesn't let enough moisture escape. If you're one of those people perpetually plagued with soggy feet, there's a third possibility. You can get the rubber-bottomed, leather-topped L.L. Bean Maine Hunting Shoe with felt liners in them. They'll allow more breathability than all rubber boots. They're heavier, more expensive, and a little rougher on the webbing, but they'll help prevent weeds from sprouting between your toes.

Walking on Snowshoes

Walking on snowshoes is not much different than just plain walking. Your larger "shoe" size, though, requires you to do two things: First, you must lift one snowshoe high enough to clear the other. You can't use a shuffling gait, but neither must you exaggerate your movements. Second, your stride must be long enough for your moving shoe to clear your stationary shoe. Otherwise you'll step on your own toe. Although the stride needed for most snowshoes is somewhat longer than usual, it isn't uncomfortable.

• *Turns*—For gradual turns, simply make a series of diagonal steps

Walking on showshoes is not much more difficult than walking on regular shoes.

in the most desired direction. To do an about-face, turn one shoe—either one—so that its toe ends up where the heel was, that's a difference of 180 degrees, sort of like assuming the fifth position in ballet. You'll want to be limber for this kick turn, but it isn't as difficult as it sounds.

• *Going Uphill*—You can walk straight up moderate hills. But when the hills get steep, you'll have to traverse—that is, zig-zag back and forth across the slope's face. This means traveling further to get to the top, but it makes climbing easier. In traversing, the downhill edge of your snowshoes will tend to tilt down hill, particularly if your snowshoes are wide. Compensate for this tendency by putting weight on the uphill side of your foot and giving a slight uphill push as you place it against the snow. That push will help pack out a flat area to support your weight.

• *Going Downhill*—As in going up, you can tackle moderate descents straight on, keeping weight on your heels. Traverse steeper grades or try skiing them. You *can* ski sometimes on snowshoes, although you increase the wear on the webbing. You'll get a stuttering slide because the gliding surface of a snowshoe leaves something to be desired. Also the tips like to dig under, so keep your weight back on those heels.

• *Outriggers*—Snowshoes offer stability. That's why they're the choice of many people who want to head for the winter trails with packs on their backs. Stability can be improved further, however, by the use of one or two ski poles. They're like outriggers and can be especially helpful in steep country or when you're carrying an unusually heavy pack.

Selecting Ski Gear

Waxable Skis

For centuries, touring skis were made only of wood. That has changed. Fiberglass skis were frowned upon only a few decades ago. Then in 1974 they started winning big in the international racing circuits. Now they're the bulk of the cross-country skis sold.

The modern glass ski is lighter, more durable, easier to wax, and easier to maintain than a wood ski. Most important, a glass ski can perform better on the trail. This is not to say that top-quality wood skis are obsolete or that they'll make you miserable on a winter trip. But if you are in the market for new skis, you'd better take a long hard look at what's available in glass before you make your choice.

Traditional materials nowadays are hard and soft woods formed in a box construction with hard wood surrounding a soft wood core. The top, bottom, and sides of good wood skis are usually made of hickory, with thin strips of beech along the edges of the bottom. The core is usually spruce or poplar.

In glass skis, there's a long list of synthetic materials that are either bonded together in layers or have a box construction around a central core. Core materials may be acryl, polyurethane, or PVC. Carbon fiber or fiberglass is used in the structural layers. The ski base is made of polyethylene or polypropylene, and tops and sidewalls are usually ABS.

The desired characteristics of a good backpackers' touring ski, whether wood or glass, are the same. You'll want a ski that is durable and maneuverable in addition to having good flotation and light weight.

• *Durability*—When you're ten miles from the nearest road, the last thing you need is a ski with a broken tip or a delaminated bottom. So don't buy skis unless they're specified as touring or mountaineering skis. Racing or light touring skis are simply not strong enough for the rough use you'll give them on a backcountry trip. With wood skis, make sure they have hickory bases and lignostone (compressed beech) edges. Mountain skis may have metal edges. In glass, look for polyethylene bases and ABS protective side walls if the ski is made with a sandwiched construction.

• *Maneuverability*—A ski that doesn't respond well will add a great deal to your fatigue. First, consider flexibility. Your ski should have a fairly flexible tip so it can follow the contour of the terrain and so it will ride on top of light snow instead of diving under it. The mid-section should be stiff enough to support your weight without really dragging its belly, yet flexible enough to give you good purchase power on the snow. The tail should be stiffer than the tip but not as stiff as the mid-section.

In addition to having bottom camber—an arc to the ski as you look at it from the side—your ski should have side camber; it should be narrower at the waist than at the tip or tail. A touring ski will be 8 to 10 mm narrower at the waist than at the tip; a mountain ski will be 10 to 12 mm narrower. The side camber helps the ski turn in the snow when you put weight on its edge while moving forward.

• *Flotation*—As with snowshoes, you need a ski that is going to keep you moving on top of the snow, not flailing around somewhere underneath it. For touring in hilly, forested country, a waist width of 52 to 60 mm is good. Once you get into those hair-raising pitches above timberline, you'll want something wider than 60 mm.

• *Weight*—By the time you find what you need in all the other qualities demanded of a good backpacking ski, you won't be able to get away with much less than 5 pounds per pair in a touring ski and 6 pounds in a mountaineering ski. The 1 pound difference between touring and mountaineering reflects the need for wider, thicker, metal-edged skis to meet the demands of very rugged terrain where alpine technique must often be used. But unless you are truly going to be mountaineering, touring skis will be just fine for your needs and much less tiring to use.

Another consideration when buying skis is length. That's something that depends on your height. With your arms raised directly above your head and the tail of the ski resting on the floor next to your foot, the ski tip should reach to your wrist.

Waxless Skis and Climbers

Perhaps it was inevitable that with the advent of fiberglass skis came the birth of waxless skis. Regular smooth-bottomed skis require the application of special waxes that allow you to push forward on the skis without slipping back but also allow you to glide. Waxless skis work on a different principle. Instead of having totally smooth bottoms, there are raised (positive) or sunken (negative) patterns along part or all of the bottom.

Trak was one of the first companies to work with the idea when it introduced its patented fishscale bottoms. The fishscale pattern protrudes from the bottom of the ski with the scales pointing toward the tail. You can push the ski forward without slipping back with this arrangement, but the ski will also glide. Another type of positive-base waxless ski uses mohair strips with the mohair angled toward the tail. Negative pattern bases that work on the same principle include diamond, bell, crescent, and step patterns. Negative-base skis tend to have less grip than positive bases because their sunken patterns require more active pushing into the snow.

As a group, waxless skis cannot perform as well as skis requiring wax. Patterned bottoms understandably slow down forward glide. But a backpacker who's breaking trail through deep, unskied snow isn't going to be too concerned with forward glide. Also these skis can save you a great deal of frustration when it comes to skiing in areas of widely varying snow conditions that would otherwise require you to use many different waxes during the course of the day. Take, for example, the West in the spring. You often find slush in the sun and crust in the shade. And in the Pacific Northwest and the Northeast, snow conditions are maddeningly erratic at almost any time.

I believe that short-tempered, impatient people would be well ad-

If your temper has a fast fuse, you'd be wise to use waxless skis, but carry a can of anti-icing spray for those times when the temperature is likely to change quickly.

vised to buy waxless skis. There's nothing that raises your ire quite so fast as a pair of skis that dump you on your tail at every step. Nearly as anger-provoking are skis that collect so much snow that they behave like sodden logs. I've seen people reduced to tears and incoherent babblings by such skis, and I'm sure that was not what they were looking for when they decided it would be fun to go skiing.

Despite the virtues of waxless skis, there are times when they do need some base preparation. They tend to ice up in quickly changing temperatures. Under these conditions, you should cover the bottoms with the antiicing sprays that are available for both patterned and mohair-bottomed skis.

Another nonwax option for skiers who want to have positive grip on steep slopes is the use of climbing skins or treads. Mohair climbing skins, which can be easily attached to ski bottoms, are fairly expensive and start at widths of about 62mm. So they can be used only on mountaineering skies. However, there's a new, inexpensive climber called "ski treads" put out by WildFlower Designs. They consist of prespliced loops of ¼-inch woven-plastic cord which slip over your skis to form "X"-shaped treads. They have little forward glide, but I've used them to go up some pretty steep hills in deep snow. The cord tends to stretch, so they do require occasional adjusting.

Bindings

The strength of a binding is as important as the strength of a ski. I was once skiing with a companion within sight of our car when his binding broke. It took two hours of laborious thrashing to get back to the vehicle. In the boondocks, that incident could have been disastrous.

• *Pin Bindings*—These are the type that clamp the toes of your boots to toe plates that have protruding pins in them. They are suitable on touring skis, provided the bindings are made of heavy-duty aluminum. Light aluminum or plastic models aren't strong enough.

• *Cable Bindings*—Cable bindings should be used on mountaineering skis, and some skiers prefer them instead of pin bindings for touring skis because of their added strength and support. A simple cable binding consists of a toe plate that fits over the edge of your boot sole and a cable that attaches to the toe plate, goes around your heel, and is cinched down with a throw clamp at the side. A heavier-duty cable binding has an adjustable toe plate and throw clamp at the front. Most of these come with lugs that are screwed into the sides of your skis to hold the cables and your heels onto the ski for downhill runs. When you buy cable bindings, make sure they have a safety heel release. Broken legs on backcountry ski trips are not recommended.

Boots

• *Touring Boots*—Regular touring-style cross-country ski boots should be worn with touring skis. These will have pin holes in the toe of the soles and are suitable for pin or cable bindings. The boots should be cut above the ankle for proper support and warmth. Avoid the light, skimpy boots used for racing. Make sure you get a pair with top-grade leather uppers that have been double stitched. They should bend easily under the ball of your foot for comfortable skiing action. But they should be fairly stiff when you hold the heel and twist the toe, otherwise you won't have good support when you edge your ski into a turn.

There are several approaches to keeping your feet warm with touring boots. Some skiers like to buy fleece-lined boots, which are fine until they get wet inside. Then the lining takes forever to dry. You can get rubber overboot socks for use in really sloppy snow, but some moisture will still form from condensation. Pullover boot socks made of polyester pile are also available, yet even these will remain effective only in dry snow. Probably your best bet is the use of good, breathable gaiters with boots that are large enough to accommodate two heavy pairs of wool socks. When it really gets wet, use the rubber socks too.

• *Mountaineering Boots*—If you are working with mountaineering skis and heavy cable bindings, it's time to switch to hiking boots or ski mountaineering boots. Ski mountaineering boots are similar to hiking boots but have felt or leather inner boots for extra warmth. Either hiking or mountaineering boots are considerably heavier than touring boots, so don't use them unless you are really forced into heavy-duty equipment by heavy-duty mountains.

Poles

Although a broken pole in the outback isn't as bad as a broken ski, it sure raises hell with the rhythm of your stride. So you should select poles made of a material that can take the weight of pushing you and your gear uphill. Bamboo poles are inexpensive and relatively strong, and ski tourers have used them for years. They have been known to break though. High-quality aluminum or fiberglass is a better bet. The poles should have adjustable wrist straps so they can be used comfortably with bare hands or with big mittens. Baskets should be 4½ to 5 inches in diameter. Most important, the poles should be the right length. An easy way to get a good fit is to stand in your stocking feet on a hard surface. Put the tip of the pole on the floor. If the top of the grip comes to your armpit, you've got the right size.

Waxes and Waxing

If you decide to go with waxable skis, you'll have to learn something about waxing. In the past, that has been the aspect of cross-country skiing surrounded by an aura of mystery. It need not be. I must admit that under snow conditions that hover right around 32°F., finding the right wax or combination of waxes can be frustrating. But most of the time waxing isn't the problem it's made out to be.

The theory behind waxes and waxing is that you should select a wax that will provide purchase on the snow when you push off but also allow the ski to slide once the push-off is made. What happens is that snow crystals stick into the wax and give you the initial grabbing power. Then once your ski is set in motion, friction disintegrates the crystals and makes a smooth surface—actually a microscopic film of water—to slide on.

The waxes themselves run from very hard to very soft. Hard waxes are simply called hard waxes and come in small lead or plastic containers. Soft waxes are called klisters and usually come in tubes, although some of the harder klisters come in lead.

Don't get cold feet when you first glimpse the wide array of waxes available; there may be ten to fifteen different kinds from one company. However, I've been skiing in the Rocky Mountain states for years and have discovered that hard green, blue, and red waxes handle just about anything but spring snow. In New England, hard green, hard blue, and blue klister, to handle icy crust, cover about three quarters of the snow conditions. In addition, many wax manufacturers have come out with simplified waxing systems that use only two or three basic waxes for all snow situations.

The trick is to start simple. If you can begin ski touring on cold new snow, you can get the feel of waxing and what wax does for you without having to hassle with complicated combinations. Straightforward snow conditions will bolster your confidence and prepare you for handling trickier situations. Waxing is not all guess work. Wax manufacturers provide waxing charts that are color coded. There is, however, some variation among different brands of wax, so try to work with one brand and get to know the characteristics of that line.

• *Applying Base Waxes*—Wood-bottomed skis require a tar-like wax, commercially called Grundvalla, as a base for other waxes and to prevent the wood from soaking up moisture. Twenty five years ago,

Don't let the profusion of waxes confuse you. Two or three waxes wisely chosen will usually get you through 75% of the snow conditions you'll encounter.

when I started cross-country skiing, we used Dixie Pine Tar instead. I'm still using it. Pine tar is available in many ski shops and in some hardware stores. Its pungent smell elicits a Pavlovian response in most cross-country skiers who use wooden skis; one smell and you know you'll soon be easing onto the snowy trails.

Grundvalla and pine tar are applied in the same way. Lay skis bottomside up on a sawhorse or chair, with their tails against something solid like a wall so they don't slip when you apply the wax. Put newspaper under the skis to catch drips. You'll need a small propane torch with a fan nozzle (to spread the flame) and a rag. Apply a small amount of base wax, and touch it with the flame until it starts to bubble. Then rub it into the wood with a rag. You have to be careful not to burn the wood itself. Beginners tend to put on too much wax and not enough heat. That tactic will cause a sticky mess. You'll have to apply more heat and wipe off the excess. When done properly, waxing should leave almost no sticky feeling to the skis.

Some skiers put on another wax called Grundvax over the Grundvalla or pine tar. It's supposed to act as a binder for the running waxes (the hard waxes and the klisters), but I've never found it necessary with pine tar.

On glass skis, the base operation is somewhat different. Instead of using pine tar, you apply paraffin or alpine-type base wax to the bottoms, except for a 24-inch section beneath the bindings. Heat the bar of wax against a 140-145°F. iron, and let the wax drip along the ski base. Then smooth the wax out by moving the iron directly along the ski bottom. After the wax is cool, use a plastic scraper to reduce the wax to a thin layer. Finish by smoothing out this layer with a waxing cork. If you'll be skiing long distances, you may want to add a plastic-base binder wax before applying the running waxes.

• *Applying Hard Waxes*—Since you can put a softer wax over a harder one but not the reverse, start by selecting the hardest wax you think will work for the expected snow conditions. For example, if you believe the conditions are borderline between green and blue, put the green on first and try to ski with that.

To apply these waxes, peel back a small strip of the lead container or push on the bottom of the plastic container and rub the wax on a two-foot section of the ski bottom beneath your binding. Try a light coat at first, and smooth it out with the palm of your hand or a waxing cork. The wax should have a shine to it when you finish.

If this doesn't work, try another coat of the same wax but don't smooth it out so much. The thicker the coat and the less you rub it, the more it will behave like the next softer wax. When several coats of the same wax fail, try an 8-to-12-inch "kicker" of the next softer wax on

Hard waxes can be smoothed out with your hand or a waxing cork, but soft waxes (klisters) are too sticky for this approach.

the bottom directly under your foot. If even this fails, you have really miscalculated the snow conditions. You should start the whole process over again using the wax you've tried as a kicker. In any event, don't give up on a wax until you've tried it for at least 150 to 200 yards; you have to "run in" the wax before it starts working properly.

• *Applying Klister*—This is sticky business, but it's part of the ski-touring ritual for many people. It's easiest to apply these soft waxes indoors where both wax and skis are warm. Half a tube of klister will do one pair of skis. Dab the wax the full length of the ski, and then rub it smooth with your hand or the applicator supplied with the wax. If you use your hand, it will feel as though you smeared it in pine pitch; wax remover or an abrasive hand cleaner will remove the mess. You can also heat the applied wax with a torch and smooth it with a paint brush. Or melt the klister in a tin can beforehand and then paint it on.

The use of klister on the trail is a different matter. It becomes cantankerous when it's cold. Most skiers carry a torch to soften the wax when they think they'll have to apply it while on a tour. But with the use of some real muscle, it's possible to rub klister smooth with your hand and save some weight in your pack.

• *Removing Wax*—At some point you'll end up with such a conglomeration of different waxes on your skis that they won't work under any conditions. It's time to take it all off. A scraper will take some of it off; a torch and scraper will take most of it off, and a scraper plus wax remover will take all of it off.

General Ski-Touring Technique

Folks who have never been on skis before would do well to find some professional help. Ski schools and ski clubs usually offer instruction in cross-country as well as alpine skiing. Sporting stores in many areas give clinics in cross-country technique. It's a good way for them to get you hooked so you'll buy equipment and also a good way for you to try the sport *before* you buy any gear. At any rate, get professional coaching if you possibly can.

The next best thing is to ask someone who already cross-skis to give you some pointers.

The following brief explanation of technique will not make you an expert. You'll be master of all terrains only after many spills and a lot of huffing and puffing. But even by working on your own, you should be able to reach the point where you can enjoy skiing with a pack over moderate terrain without difficulty.

The keys to success: relax, don't get frustrated, and enjoy it all—even the falls.

Okay. Start by finding a flat spot after a new snow on a "green" or "blue" day. In other words, the temperature is between 18°F. and 30°F. Put on green or blue wax. The containers and the temperature will tell you which one.

• *Shuffle*—Now, put on your skis and shuffle. Just slide one foot forward and then the other, using poles for balance. If you're like most people, as your right ski slides forward your left arm will swing forward to plant the ski pole for balance. It's usually an automatic reaction, and it's the right reaction for proper balance.

• *Step Turn*—After shuffling around a bit, try turning. Pick up your left ski; angle it to the left, and put it down. Bring your right ski up alongside your left ski. Repeat the process until you're headed back the way you came. This is called a step turn. Try the same thing to the right.

• *Glide*—Once you're accustomed to the feel of having skis on and have gotten a sense of balance, you'll realize that you feel most stable with your skis placed from 5 to 6 inches apart. Now you can stop shuffling and start gliding. Push off with one ski and glide forward on the other; it's similar to ice skating except you don't have to angle the ski to get the push.

• *Pole Push*—As you practice the glide, continue to use the poles for balance, and also try using them for additional push. Angle the pole slightly to your rear and place it in the snow in a line that falls just behind the heel of your boot. By pushing back on the pole in this position, you'll add a great deal more power to your glide. As your pole arm follows through to the rear, let that arm and hand relax. The wrist strap will hold the pole from falling, and you won't get worn out as quickly.

• *Going Uphill*—Eventually you'll get bored with the flats, which means you're ready for the hills. You can glide right up moderate hills if you've done a good waxing job. On steeper hills, you'll be forced to shift down to a shuffle. Steeper grades require you to change from a direct uphill course to a zig-zag, or traverse.

When the going gets really rough, you may have to herringbone to keep from sliding backwards. In this technique, you angle both ski tips out, as if you were badly splayfooted and bowlegged at the same time. Then you walk uphill. The herringbone feels awkward and is tiring, but it keeps you going uphill.

As a final resort, short of climbers, use the side step. With skis angled across the face of the hill, step sideways and dig the uphill edges of your skis into the snow. This is a really slow method, yet it's good for almost anything except a cliff.

Going up requires muscle and lung power along with good balance and technique. But it's a prerequisite for the excitement of coming down.

• *Going Downhill*—Start on a little hill, one that has a clear flat runout at the bottom. Better yet, choose one that merges into an uphill grade at the bottom to slow and stop you. Push off and go straight down. Keep your skis comfortably apart. Bend your knees a little and weight your skis evenly. Hold the poles out in front of you and spread out a bit from your body. If you fall, get up and start down again. Try coming straight down four or five times.

Once you're accustomed to the sensation of skiing, make a step turn as you descend. It's done the same way you do it on the flat, but you'll have to quicken the steps. Turn far enough to end up heading uphill and stopping. Practice straight runs and step turns on the little hill until you feel comfortable. Then tackle a bigger hill and do the same thing.

• *Kick Turn*—As the downhill pitch increases, you'll find you can slow your descent by skiing across the hill instead of going straight down. When you want to stop, you just turn your skis uphill. At the end of each zig across the hill, however, you must get turned around so you can zag. This is where the kick turn comes in. Put the heel of your downhill ski in the snow next to the tip of your uphill ski so that the downhill ski is sticking up in the air. Now, swing the tip of that ski in an arc that comes down next to the heel of your uphill ski. You're halfway through the turn and in a very awkward position. Okay, swing your uphill ski around and bring it down parallel to the other and pointing in the same direction. Your uphill ski has just become your downhill ski. You're ready to zag.

The poles come in very handy for balance while you're doing this turn. And although the whole process sounds complicated and muscle pulling, you get the hang of it pretty quickly.

• *Snowplow*—A third turn, the snowplow, can be used when you want to make a series of turns without stopping. For this one, angle the heels of your skis out and the tips in so they form a "V." Pull your knees in toward each another, throwing weight onto the skis' inside edges and forcing them to angle into the snow. On gentle slopes, you can bring yourself to a stop using this position. The wider the angle of the "V" and the more you slant the inside ski edges into the snow, the slower you'll go. To turn, throw more weight on one ski than on the other by leaning out over that ski. You'll turn in the direction of the weighted ski.

• *Brakes*—The snowplow comes in very handy on narrow trails where you don't have enough room to slow down by turning or traversing; there are some other methods of braking too. You can hold

A snowplow may be the sign of a real beginner on the groomed ski slopes, but it's standard operational procedure for the cross-country skier.

both ski poles between your legs with one hand holding the handles in front of you and the other hand holding the shafts between your legs mid-way down the poles. With your knees bent sharply, apply upward pressure with your upper hand and downward pressure with the hand holding the shafts. The baskets and tips of the poles drag and bite into the snow, slowing you down; the more pressure applied the slower you go.

A variation on this friction-brake technique is to bend down so you're hunkering on the skis and using your hands with your fingers pointing to the rear as a drag. Just let the poles trail behind from their wrist straps. If you really get roaring down a hill and your hands don't provide enough drag, apply your rear end to the snow. You'll stop, and this technique is quite acceptable; grace is not the sign of an experienced ski tourer. Sometimes you're glad to get down a mountain any way you can.

Using the techniques described here, you can handle any situation encountered in general touring. There are more refined and fancy ways to turn and stop, which you may develop if you really get into this method of winter travel. But the basics are here, and that's where you must start.

The old friction-brake technique can get you through many a tough place.

Besides, even without finely tuned skills, you can still ski to within sight of feeding deer or find the ludicrous waddle marks made by porcupines moving across the snow.

If you're careful, there's no reason you can't put on your pack and ski away from the winter confines of enclosed houses for a trip of several days. At no other time will the air feel so clean or snow crystals glitter on branches with quite such dazzling intensity. Even snowstorms will become more palpable to your senses once you've made the committment to live outside with them. And when the snow stops, the winter scene becomes a surprise of subtle shapes, colors, and sounds.

Some Final Notes on Skis and Snowshoes

• Don't use skis or snowshoes as bridges to span streams or ditches; your weight could break them.

• Avoid stepping on snow-covered logs and branches when traversing hillsides; they're slippery and can land you on your tail.

• Watch for under-snow snags, particularly when going downhill; if you catch a tip, you'll probably go on your nose.

• Be careful of "frozen" lakes and streams; they may not be.

• Rotate the task of trail-breaking with your companions.

• Take a good snowshoe or ski repair kit when you head into the backcountry.

Snowshoe Repair:	*Ski Repair:*
Wire	Plastic or aluminum emergency ski tip
Pliers	One complete set of binding parts
Rawhide thongs	Combination tool (pliers, screwdriver, wrench,
Pocket knife	wirecutters in one)

And a Few Words on Carrying Your Gear

The exterior-frame pack that's so efficient for hikers and even snowshoers is a horror for skiers. These packs carry the weight too high for proper balance when you're skiing. Instead, you'll want to use one of the internal-frame rucksacks or one of the soft, body-contour packs. A number of internal-frame packs utilize rigid or semi-flexible frames made of aluminum, fiberglass, or plastic. They keep the weight low and close to your back, where you'll want it for stability. The body-contour packs have no frames and rely on their shapes, when properly

When you're on skis, a soft pack that conforms to the contours of your body is much more stable than an external-frame pack.

packed, to conform to your own back contours. These can be extremely effective. The one I use is called the Terraplane and is made by Kletterwerks. It's a large-volume pack with well-thought-out design features.

If you must use an exterior-frame pack, attach the pack bag to the frame at the lowest point possible, and distribute the weight so it rides low and close to your back.

Some winter campers use sleds or toboggans to transport their gear, and this can be a good way to handle things on level terrain. But in the hills, you're always straining to pull them up behind you or fighting to hold them back on downgrades. Besides, when you're using skis, managing a sled ruins the joyous freedom of being able to curve down through a steep slope of deep, light powder.

In the end, skis are more than a means of getting there.

12

Cold-Weather Hazards

Frostbite

I suppose we've all felt the teeth of a cold day. Perhaps it's late and we've been snowshoeing all afternoon without anything to eat. The sun has gone down; the temperature drops. Our toes begin to tingle, and our fingers start to ache. A warm house or even a car heater is a welcome relief.

Yet even the average snowshoer or cross-country skier won't always be able to rely on the convenience of a house or a car to warm cold toes, fingers, and ears. At some point, cold is going to bite when you're out in the boondocks. Your feet will get wet and start to chill, and then really painful cold will set in. You've got to do something. You can't ignore the discomfort. If you do, you'll likely end up with frostbite.

Frostbite is the formation of ice crystals between the cells of your body tissue. These ice crystals are formed from water that has actually been drawn from your cells. What makes frostbite so damaging to your body tissue is this dehydration of the cells along with the absence of the blood's oxygen and nourishment.

The mechanism that causes frostbite is related to your circulatory system. As arteries carry fresh blood away from your heart to your extremities and skin, they become small and are called arterioles. The arterioles supply blood to even smaller blood passageways called capillaries. It is through the capillaries' walls that oxygen and nourishment are transferred directly to the surrounding tissues. When blood reaches the end of a network of capillaries, it enters what is called a venule, which then connects to a vein and carries the blood back to your heart.

It's a rather intricate and amazing system. But problems occur with this circulatory process when too much chilling takes place in a localized area—a soggy toe in a tight boot, for example. In an attempt to prevent continued cooling of the blood, and therefore the entire body, the arterioles involuntarily shut off their flow to the capillaries in the cold extremity. Instead of flowing through the capillary network, blood is sent through a shortcut, called a capillary shunt, directly to a venule. The affected area, totally deprived of any heat, actually starts to freeze.

In the case of "superficial frostbite," the bitten area will look white and may feel hard, but firm pressure will indicate underlying resilience. "Deep frostbite" sinks far into skin tissue and even bones, causing extreme damage. Before the area is thawed, it will feel as hard and unpliable as any frozen meat you take from a freezer. Not very pleasant.

Despite the grim consequences that frostbite can have—the loss of a toe or a finger—proper clothing, nourishment, and some cold-weather sense can all but eliminate your chances of being badly bitten.

Frostbite is most likely to happen to feet, hands, or face—to feet and hands because they're so far from the heart, to the face because it's often left exposed to the weather. For all these areas, what you wear is the first line of defense.

Feet are the hardest to protect. They're often beneath snow that can be quite a bit colder below the surface than it is on top. When you wear hiking or cross-country ski boots, make sure they're properly treated with a waterproofing compound and that they fit well. A tight boot will restrict blood circulation, and that's exactly what you don't want to do. Two pairs of wool socks should be a minimum with these boots. And if it's really cold, a pair of regular or insulated gaiters (one size fits all) or overboots (small, medium, or large) will add further protection.

For hands your best bet is wool mittens with waterproof overmitts. Make sure they come far enough up your arms to overlap your sleeves. Thin silk glove liners should be worn underneath (see page 144).

Protecting your face is a bit more difficult. A wool or acrylic hat that

Strange as it may seem, putting on a hat and pulling up your hood will help keep your hands and feet warm.

you can pull down over your ears and a parka hood you can close so that only your eyes are exposed are the two most common forms of insulation. In extreme cold, a leather face mask will give you more protection.

Although feet, hands, and face are most prone to frostbite, the rest of your body needs adequate protection too. The old adage that says, "If your feet are cold, put on your hat and another sweater" makes a lot of sense. The more heat you can conserve in your torso, the warmer your extremities will stay. Polyester insulation with a good wind parka and wind pants makes an effective combination.

Equally as important as what you wear is what you eat. Good food with a high-calorie count is essential for your body's heat-producing mechanism.

Proper food and clothing will help prevent frostbite, but what you do on the trail and in camp is also important. Panting, for instance, can be responsible for a great deal of heat loss through your lungs. So you should take special care to avoid a lot of huffing and puffing.

Smoking and drinking alcohol present other dangers when frostbite is a possibility. Smoking restricts your capillaries and therefore slows the circulation of blood to your extremities and the surface of your skin. Alcohol, by contrast, dilates your vascular system, causing increased blood flow at the surface of your skin. There it gets chilled and results in a reduction of your entire body's temperature. Don't suppose that butts and booze will cancel the effects of one another, either. They won't.

Despite all your precautions, don't assume you're immune to the dangers of frostbite. Whenever your extremities start to feel cold and uncomfortable, do something about it. If toes or fingers suddenly *stop* feeling cold and uncomfortable, the frost may have already bitten.

A good treatment for cold feet is to take off your boots and socks and warm your feet by pressing them firmly with warm hands. If there is any chance that superficial frostbite has already occurred, *do not rub* the affected area. Rubbing will only increase damage to the injured tissue. More effective, but rather uncomfortable for a companion, is to put your feet on a buddy's belly. When your feet have been warmed, you should put on dry socks before you don boots again.

Hands are more easily warmed and can be placed in your own armpits or crotch. Once hands are warmed, they can be used to warm your ears and face, as well as feet.

A sure danger sign on your face is the appearance of white blotches. Keep a close eye on companions for this frostbite indicator.

It's ironic that in all but cases of superficial frostbite (or frostnip as it's often called), the best first aid on the trail is to do nothing at all. The most effective known treatment for frostbite is rapid rewarming in water that can be kept at a temperature between 108°F. and 112°F. while the affected area is immersed for 20 to 30 minutes. But this method is effective only if the patient can remain warm, quiet, and comfortable while recovering afterward.

Walking on thawed feet, for instance, would not only be excruciatingly painful but also would do a great deal more damage to injured tissue. So if warmth and comfort are not available for a long-term recovery, don't attempt to thaw an area of deep frostbite. Get the patient to permanent shelter and to professional medical attention as soon as possible. Walking on frozen feet seems to do no additional harm, and there are records of people who have traveled on their own for up to two and three days in this state.

The main point, of course, is to avoid such a necessity. So pay careful attention to your clothes and food, and develop some sensible cold-weather savvy.

Avalanche

Although snow is often the foundation of winter shelters, winter transportation, and awe-inspiring scenery, it's also—under certain conditions—one of winter's greatest hazards. Every year, avalanches take their toll of unwary winter travelers, most of whom are themselves responsible for triggering the slide that buries them.

Despite the research that has been done on avalanches, the intricate forces that cause them are still not entirely understood. Fallen snow is constantly going through changes (or metamorphoses) that influence its stability—its ability or lack of ability to be cohesive and to bond to other layers of snow within a snow pack. Much of this metamorphosis is caused by basic changes in the snow crystals themselves—in their shapes, structure, water content, and so forth. But changes in stability are also influenced by surface snow conditions; by each successive layer of snow that falls throughout the winter; and by temperature, wind velocity, and snow depth. Although the whys and wherefores of avalanches are extremely complex, there are some general considerations that the winter camper should be familiar with in order to cope wisely with this hazard.

Types of Avalanches

There are two general types of avalanches.

• A loose-snow avalanche starts over a very small area but grows and spreads out in a fanlike fashion during its descent. As its name implies, there is little cohesion to the snow in this type of slide.

• Starting over a large area all at once, a slab avalanche is distinguished by a definite fracture line, which can be seen where the sliding snow breaks away from the rest of the snow pack. This type of slide starts as a slab but may break up as it move downslope.

Contributing Weather and Snow Conditions

Both weather and snow conditions have an influence on avalanche danger. A high percentage of avalanches occur during or shortly after a storm, particularly if the weather patterns are changing rapidly. The avalanche danger increases even more when snow is blown by winds of 15 mph or more and when snow accumulations exceed one inch per hour. Campers should be especially watchful if new snow exceeds a depth of one foot. If this snow is dry, it won't bond as well as wet snow and therefore is prone to slide more easily.

The type of snow cover already on the ground can influence avalanche danger too. When old snow becomes deep enough to cover boulders and bushes that might help hold snow in place, danger increases. In addition, smooth snow such as sun-melted crusts or surfaces like those caused by wind pack are less likely to hold new snow than are rough surfaces.

Contributing Slope Conditions.

Avalanches are most common on slopes of 30 to 45 degrees. Yet large avalanches do occur on slopes as gentle as 25 degrees and as steep as 65 degrees. Steeper pitches usually don't hold enough snow to pose a problem. Slopes that are smooth and open are more dangeorus than those covered with rocks, trees, and bushes, which can act as anchors to hold snow in place. The shape of an incline is important. Convex slopes are more likely to avalanche than concave slopes.

The direction a slope faces is another contributing factor. Because north-facing slopes tend to be covered with dry, light snow especially in midwinter, this is the time they're most likely to slide. South-facing slopes, on the other hand, are more hazardous in the spring when melt water seeps into the snow pack and causes unstable conditions. Finally, lee slopes are more dangerous than slopes exposed to the wind. Greater amounts of snow pile up on lee slopes, often forming overhanging snow cornices that can break off and trigger an avalanche.

Danger Signs

Although avalanches can occur at any time, there are some definite things you should watch for. Avoid any areas that show signs of past avalanche activity. Where a forested area suddenly opens into a treeless chute, you should detour. Sometimes these chutes will contain young trees that all bend downslope—an indication of past avalanches. Recent slide activity is a warning that you should be par-

Open areas below steep chutes suggest prime avalanche areas, especially when interspersed with new tree growth.

ticularly watchful. Even when large avalanches aren't visible, just the sight of snowballs rolling down a slope is enough to indicate danger. Beware, too, when the snow seems to crack or settle suddenly under your skis or snowshoes.

Route Selection

When you travel in avalanche country, wise route selection is imperative. Under no circumstances should you cross a potential slide area when there is another way around. Look for a route that takes you through heavily forested areas or stay well out from the bottom of a slope and in the center of a valley. When you're on a ridge, stay on the windward side. If you must cross an exposed slope, do it as close to the top as possible.

Precautions

I remember a frightening March morning many years ago when I poked my head from the entrance of a snow cave at 11,000 feet and found prime avalanche conditions. During the night, more than a foot of new, dry powder had fallen onto an old snow base that was hard and smooth. As if that weren't bad enough, we were high above timberline and had to descend several miles of steep slopes before we reached the safety of a forested area. You can be sure that we took every precaution before pushing off into that new snow.

First, we donned hats and mittens and secured all closures on our clothing. If anyone did get caught in a slide, we wanted to have as much body protection as possible. Each one of us also tied an avalanche cord around his waist. These rigs consist of 50 feet of red nylon cord to which numbered aluminum clips are affixed at intervals of one meter. If one of us should be buried by an avalanche, the light cord would ride to the surface of the snow, where it would tell rescuers the victim's location and depth.

Before starting down the mountain, we took the ski-pole straps off our wrists and undid the waist and sternum straps on our packs so that we improved our chances to get rid of this gear if necessary.

Then, one at a time, we skied straight downhill until we reached the relative safety of rock outcroppings. Whoever skied down the slope was carefully watched by the others. If a slide did catch someone, we wanted to be able to pinpoint the location.

Fortunately, we all descended without a mishap but not without considerable suspense.

Avalanche!

I've never been caught in a avalanche. Friends of mine who have say it's a terrifying experience.

The theory is that you should try to ski or snowshoe out of the slide's path. If this becomes impossible, you try to jettison skis, poles, and pack. Then you use a breaststroke or backstroke in an attempt to stay toward the surface of the snow. Before coming to rest, you should try to make a breathing space in the snow by bringing your arms up around your face. After this, you must concentrate very, very hard on not panicking.

It must be hard. My friends say that they were buried before they knew what hit them, that snow was packed around them so solidly they couldn't move an inch, and that they had no idea what direction was up and what was down. Trying to dig yourself out of a situation like this would be futile unless you were sure you were very close to the surface and you knew where the surface was. It's better to do as my friends did and conserve what air was available while praying that campanions would come to the rescue.

Rescue

Rescue measures must start immediately. After one hour, a person buried in the snow has only a 50 percent chance of survival. If you are the only rescuer present, don't go off in search of help. Go to the last spot you saw the victim, and look for his avalanche cord there and downhill. If no cord was worn, or if it can't be found, start probing the snow with a ski pole or a sectional aluminum avalanche probe. Probe in a systematic manner at intervals of one or two feet, starting at the point the victim disappeared. The area you probe should fan out as you descend the slope. The more searchers you have probing, the greater the chances of locating the victim quickly. When more than one person is at the scene, someone should go for help if it's nearby.

When a victim is dug out of the snow, first check for breathing. If necessary, apply mouth-to-mouth respiration. Wrap the person in dry clothes or a sleeping bag and treat him for shock by keeping him lying down with his feet elevated. Check for cuts and broken bones.

Much better by far than having to go through any heroics is to make sure you and your companions stay on top of the snow where you can enjoy the view. If you must end up beneath the stuff, do it only in the comfortable confines of a well-wrought snow cave.

SECTION IV

Camping
in Mixed Weather

13

From One Extreme
to Another,
on the Same Trip

It all started innocently enough. The trailhead was amidst giant saguaro cactus, teddybear chollas, and wispy ocotillo. Heat from the midday sun had made us strip to light shirts. Even then, as we began to climb Tanque Verde Ridge, the air seemed a bit too hot.

By the time lunch was on our minds, however, we'd hiked above the saguaro, and a growing breeze had put a chill in the air. Sweaters and the lee of a large boulder went well with our sausage and cheese. At dinner time, after 7 miles of hiking and a 3,000-foot increase in elevation, we were remote from desert vegetation and surrounded by a juniper forest. Shirts and sweaters were covered by more shirts. Even a wool hat and mittens felt none too warm as I downed the last cup of coffee before climbing into the protection of our mountain tent, pitched amidst patches of snow left from a recent storm.

In ten hours we had experienced a range of temperatures wide enough to include every season of the year in most parts of the U.S. That hike for all seasons happened to be near Tucson, Arizona, during the first week in April. But there are any number of places and times across the continent in which a hike of a few hours or days will take you through an extremely wide variety of weather conditions.

In many cases, the changing weather can be linked to changes in elevation. Because of decreasing atmospheric pressure, air is cooled as it pushes up mountain sides. Dry air drops about 5°F. for every 1,000 feet it rises. Wet air, because of warmth given up through condensation of water vapor, drops only around 3°F. for every 1,000-foot rise. In either case, the relatively mild temperatures you experience in a valley at the start of a hike may give way to very chilly temperatures on a summit 4,000 or 5,000 feet above.

The drizzle you experience in the lowlands could change to sleet or snow while you climb. For example, as I write these words on September 11, the air temperature is 42°F. and rain is falling at my southwestern-Montana home. Yet through the clouds the snowline is visible only 300 or 400 feet above. And the top of Wheeler Mountain, where only last week I hiked in a T-shirt, is getting its first real blast of winter.

The Rockies, though, aren't the only mountains to generate such fickle weather. New Hampshire's White Mountains, particularly 6,288-foot Mt. Washington—highest point in the northeast, have some of the harshest and most unpredictable weather on our continent. Although the height of Washington is nothing compared to the Rockies or the Sierra Nevada, it consistently generates worse weather, exposed as it is to the arctic weather systems from the north and west and the tropical systems from the east and south. Fogs there can be unbelievably dense, and snow has been recorded for every month of the year. Perhaps Mt. Washington is most notorious for its winds. In 1934, the highest wind velocity ever recorded was registered on its summit. It's no wonder that trails leading into the White Mountains have signs reading, "STOP. The area ahead has the worst weather in America. Many have died there from exposure, even in the summer. Turn back now if the weather is bad."

Mountain weather anywhere can be harsh, but it can also be surprisingly local. It may not be at all unusual to have temperatures in the 80s as you hike in a valley, while rain or even snow races in horizontal sheets across a summit only a mile or two away. By contrast, low stratus clouds may cause rain or drizzle at low elevations but leave peaks in the sunshine. In addition, temperature inversions—most often experienced in the wintertime—can cause extremely cold temperatures at low elevations while the air only a few hundred feet up the slope remains relatively mild.

Wind, whether on the summit of a mountain or in the flatlands, can very quickly make one season seem like a different one. At any temperature, the air feels cooler against exposed skin when the wind blows than when the air is calm (see page 83). The stronger the wind,

You may be hot hiking in a valley though snow blows across a mountainside a few miles away at the same time.

the cooler the air will feel. For example, 50°F. does not sound very cold, and most of us have undoubtedly hiked at this temperature. But in a 30-mph wind, 50°F. feels like minus 45°F. in a dead calm. When I consider the mountain passes and the rolling plains I've crossed while leaning into "summer" winds, no wonder it's felt like winter and I've put on every stitch of clothing in my pack!

There is one wind, however, that acts in just the opposite way. Quick changes in weather, particularly in the winter, can come with chinook winds along the east slopes of the northern Rockies. Called "the snow eaters" by the Indians, a chinook brings warm, dry air that can melt snow amazingly fast, leaving cross-country skiers in a waxing quandary and their packs piled high with discarded clothes. As examples of how fast these winds can change things, consider the day in Havre, Montana, when the temperature rose 33 degrees in 3 minutes, or the time in March along Canada's Mackenzie River when 6 hours and a chinook were enough to make the thermometer go from 5°F. below zero to 54°F. above.

While a chinook can cause weather to swiftly change, the lay of the land can cause dramatic climatic turnabouts in short distances. Take the Cascade Range in the Pacific Northwest. Weather fronts rolling in from the ocean hit the western slopes of the Cascades and dump all their moisture before going over the mountaintops. Consequently, a hiker, within one day on the trail, can move from a cool, wet world of Douglas fir and western hemlock on the west slopes to the warm, dry realm of ponderosa pine on the eastern slopes.

Although many of the Dr. Jekyll-Mr. Hyde changes in weather result from elevation, wind, and geography, the transition periods between actual seasons can also be very unsettled times. The tug-of-war between spring and summer or fall and winter is notorious for bringing weather characteristic of both seasons. In the middle of April, while canoeing in southern Georgia, I've experienced calm, hot days that were immediately followed by cool, wet, and windy stretches laced with tornadoes. A Colorado September, on the other hand, can dish up snow while you're setting up camp one day and be in the 70s while you're breaking the same camp the next morning.

Even the difference between day and night can bring dramatic temperature fluctuations, especially in the desert. Where humidity is low, as much as 90% of the heat absorbed by the earth during the day is radiated back into the atmosphere at night. Because of this pattern, temperatures may vary by 50 degrees or more within a span measured in hours.

Because of the possibilities for getting into trips of all seasons, you may need to be ready to handle all the kinds of weather on the same

Depending on the whim of the weather, spring in the Great Basin Desert can be a time for parkas or sun hats.

trip. Being properly prepared with clothing and gear is essential, but having the mental attitude to deal with drastic weather changes is just as important. More than a few campers have panicked when it snowed unexpectedly or when temperatures hit the 90s on what was expected to be a mild day.

The first step in preparing your head and your gear for an all-weather trip is to know what extremes are possible. Use either the *Climatic Atlas of the U.S.* (see page 5) or a *Climatic Survey* of a specific state (see page 6) to give you this background. Then make sure you've checked the long-range weather forecast and you've brushed up on your weather-reading skills before you take off.

Planning clothes and gear for a trip of all seasons poses some definite complications. Heat, rain, snow and cold all require somewhat different approaches. In order to keep weight and bulk to a minimum, clothes and gear have to serve as many purposes as possible. The following is a run down of the clothes I take when I expect to get widely varying weather. Most of these items have been discussed in more detail elsewhere in this book (see index).

Clothing

Underwear

Wool-cotton-blend fishnet underwear with short sleeves and short pants is what I wear. The short versions of both top and bottom provides insulation to my torso while allowing me to wear shorts and short-sleeved shirts over the underwear without making me look like second cousin to Spiderman. REI's Sonora T-shirt would be a good choice here also.

Socks

A pair of light polypro inner socks plus a pair of medium to heavy wool/polypro outer socks can handle just about any weather short of the sub-zero stuff.

Footwear

On the hiking trail, nothing serves better under widely varying weather conditions than your regular hiking boots (see page 31). Make sure all the stitching is intact and that the boots are properly waterproofed before you leave on your trip. Carry waterproofing compound with you, and use it often.

When cycling, regular cycling shoes will do with a pair of water-proof booties or plastic bags to go over them when it rains.

In a canoe, I use L.L. Bean's Rubber Moccasins with removable wool-pile innersoles to slip in when the air gets cold. The rubber keeps out water, and the moccasin is low enough to allow the evaporation of sweat.

Pants

Light, loose wool pants are best, if you can stand a little warmth on a hot day. Remember that desert nomads wear loose-fitting wool garments because those are the only clothes that protect them against the extremes of daytime heat and nighttime cold. A compromise would be "tin" pants which will repel rain but won't get as hot as wool. In either case, a pair of rain chaps will add as little as 8 ounces to your pack with minimal bulk, and they'll protect you against rain, wind, and cold.

Shirt

A light-colored poplin (60% polyester, 35% cotton) shirt and a lightweight wool shirt (both with long sleeves) should cover all bases.

Jacket

A polyester pile jacket with a full-length zipper front is the only answer these days.

Hat and Mittens

If you have any doubt about what the temperature will do, take along a wool or pile hat and mittens. Last year an August thunderstorm at 9,000 feet in Wyoming left an inch of slush on my camp. I was glad I'd packed these items, and I felt prepared for the worst after I'd put them on.

Poncho

A poncho has too many advantages to be left at home.

Parka Shell

If you're going to take one (I usually do even though I have a poncho) make it breathable waterproof.

Equipment

Bivouac Sack

Although a tarp can serve as a light shelter in many situations, biting insects can make a tarp seem like a torture chamber in places like New England, where summer moisture can produce squadrons of mosquitoes. One possible solution that will add light weight and bulk to your pack is a bivouac sack. In the past, waterproof bivouac sacks had a real problem with condensation, but the recent use of breathable waterproofs has considerably reduced that problem.

A bivouac sack is a large bag designed to go over one or two sleeping bags and weighing from one pound to 2½ pounds. It will usually have pullout tabs on each side of the head section, and these can be tied to bushes, trees, or stakes to provide inside headroom. A good sack has mosquito netting in the head section and a storm flap that can be completely closed. When the night is hot, you can have the flap open and gaze at the stars. If things get feeling too cozy, lie on the top of your sleeping bag with just the sack as a cover. In rain and cold, you close the storm flap and get into your sleeping bag. The bivouac sack will increase the temperature rating of your bag by about 10°F.

To some people, a bivouac sack can seem very claustrophobic. But the best sacks have netted side vents. When the corner tabs of the sack are pulled out with guylines, those vents can remain open to give you fresh air and allow you to see out even in the rain.

Tent

A tent, of course, will give you more room and a place to store your gear. One that is light in weight and color, has plenty of ventilation with mosquito netting but still can be closed up tight with storm doors and windows will protect you against almost any weather.

Sleeping Bags

In widely varying temperature ranges, one bag can't be comfortable at all readings. But a two-bag system can be. Several companies sell this kind of system. It usually consists of a lightweight summer inner bag combined with a medium-weight spring-autumn outer bag. You can use the bags separately to finely tune your sleeping comfort for the temperatures typical of the three milder seasons, or you can use them together to cope with winter cold.

You can also make your own two-bag system by buying a lightweight (about two pounds) outer bag to go over your present sleeping bag. The outer bag, usually filled with polyester, will improve the temperature rating of your present bag by 15 to 20 degrees and you can use it alone when your regular bag is too warm. Be sure to get one with a full length zipper for maximum ventilation in hot temperatures.

Stoves

I'd take along a stove, preferably a pump variety that burns white gasoline. This type can be made to work effectively under all kinds of heat, rain, cold, and wind. A fire under widely varying conditions can be anything from uncomfortable to impossible.

Technique

As carefully as you select your clothing and gear for a trip of all seasons, it's still going to weigh more than what you usually carry. There isn't anything you can do about that when you expect to have the full gamut of weather during your trip. But sometimes you can lighten your load along the way.

The use of a cache (see page 115) is one possibility. For example, let's say you'll cross the Cascades from west to east and come back the same route. Before you start to descend the dry, warm eastern slopes, you could cache some of the clothes you use for wet, cool weather. These you could pick up again on your return trip along with the last days' food, which you could have cached to cut more weight.

Another possibility is to set up a cache before you start your trip. On a desert-mountain hike, for instance, you could drive or hike or both to a point on the route where you'd be leaving the desert and starting into the mountains. Here, you can cache cold-weather clothes, rain gear, and food that might not be needed on the first leg of the trip. This kind of arrangement can be particularly useful on desert-mountain hikes typical of places like Organ Pipe Cactus National Monument in Arizona or in Texas's Big Bend National Park.

The use of a base camp is still another way of handling the weight problem. You drive or hike with your all-weather stockpile of gear and food to a spot you want to use as a general base for hiking, biking, or canoeing. It may be at the edge of desert and mountains or it may simply be in a place or during a time of year that can serve up the whole weather works. In any event, you can operate out of this

base, making day or overnight jaunts on which you take only the clothes you'll need in order to match the short-range weather expectations.

Whatever you decide upon for the logistics of carrying, caching, or stockpiling your clothes and gear, a trip on which the weather might swing through any or all the extremes doesn't have to be a hassle. Some thoughtful planning will keep you comfortable in any weather you'll encounter. Besides, a trip through a kaleidoscope of seasons will never be dull, and it can act as an ideal "short course" in the nuances and the subtleties of harsh-weather camping.

Index